#AttackAnxiety

WINNING THE FIGHT

Don Womble

Printed in the United States of America

ISBN - 978-1-0878-8450-9
LCCN- 2020910025

10 9 8 7 6 5 4 3 2-

EMPIRE PUBLISHING

www.empirebookpublishing.com

Dedication

This book is dedicated to my immediate family.

- My Dad, John T, and my Mother Anna Mae Womble.
- My wife and best friend, Kathy Womble
- My children and their spouses:
    - Don Womble II
    - Matthew Britton and Nishia Womble
    - Anna and Dylan Cink
- My grandchildren and their spouses:
    - Kristian and Kyle Leonhardt
    - Angel and Cason Griffin
    - Bryce Womble
    - Theodore Ray Cink to be born June 2020
- My great-grandchildren:
    - Kase Dwayne Leonhardt
    - Keeton Ray Leonhardt to be born August 2020

I love each one of you more than words can express and I cherish the moments that we spend together.

Acknowledgement

This page is the most difficult page that I have attempted to write. There have been countless individuals that I should acknowledge, yet space does not permit it.

I want to mention my parents, John T. and Anna Mae Womble, both of whom are in Heaven. The two of them taught me wholesome unconditional love. My wife, Kathy, has been my soulmate, lover, advisor, and friend for nearly fifty years. I love you, my bride.

To my children, Don II, Matthew Britton, and Anna, not only am I proud of each of you, but I also want to thank you for selflessly sharing me to serve and help people while you were growing up. I love all three of you with my whole being.

My brothers brought so much enjoyment into my life. These three men are my heroes: Johnny Hilton and Archie Wayne Womble who are both in Heaven. Big brother Bennie Lewis Womble, *"we are carrying the legacy."* I cherish our times we have had together, and I love each of you forever.

I am full of gratitude to a group of individuals that promoted and planned the book-birthing celebration of #AttackAnxiety: Zak and Amanda Acker, Heather Koenig, Kashi Wallace, and Sam McKern. I must applaud Don II, Matthew Britton, and Kathy Womble, along with Anna Cink, plus Angel Griffin for the book title and the front cover inspiration.

On the spiritual side, I would not have know how to love and lead people without the example of my faithful pastor and my life mentor, Frank Johnson. I love you.

To the many staff pastors, administrators, and faithful people that have allowed me to lead them, I say thank you from the bottom of my heart. I love you. Also, I want to thank Dave Koenig for his assistance and advice in the early stages of the writing and proofreading of this book.

I want to say thank you to Sam McKern for inspiring me to write a book. My gratitude likewise goes to Jason Pelley and Bryan Saffle for encouraging me to take precious time away from the office to research and write my story.

It is important to me to thank Francesca Maria, my representative with Empire Publishing and Literary Service Bureau, for her guidance, patience, and expertise, even before we began the publishing process. A big thank you also must go to Debbie Kefke, the artist that created the drawings preceding each chapter in this composition.

You will soon discover that this book contains much of my journey, as I have learned how to handle anxiety disorders. I sincerely desire for this collection of life stories, to become a self-help resource for many fellow strugglers, who are daily managing anxiety disorders.

Contents

Chapter Twelve

About the Author

Don has earned several college degrees, with one being an MBA in Organizational Psychology and Development. In 2017, he co-founded a professional counseling center in the community where he lives. Don has achieved certification with the John Maxwell Team as a speaker, teacher, and coach. Many people know him as a church planter, pastor, and mentor. He currently serves on the board of directors for several charitable organizations.

From childhood through adult life, Don Womble, has lived with Generalized Anxiety and Panic Attacks. He is familiar with the fear and battles of those who agonize from these struggles. Don has learned by trial and error how to work through these disorders. Through the techniques and tools that he has attained, he has provided teaching, mentoring, and assistance to countless individuals suffering from the same challenges.

Don and his wife, Kathy, and family live in the south Fort Worth, Texas area. He considers himself a family man and enjoys family events more than any activities.

Preface

You cannot go through your life avoiding social interactions and awkward situations. These things are necessary aspects of one's life. Admittedly, everyone struggles with them to varying degrees. What might be a momentary embarrassment to someone in a certain context might be lifelong devastation for another. This gives rise to a number of mental health-related issues – including anxiety.

Managing anxiety is a challenging task, especially on an individual level. This is despite the fact that knowing how to manage anxiety on an individual level is the most important skill you can have – both for yourself and for those around you.

This book is a journey that will arm you the necessary tools to not just confront, but manage your anxiety. To do that, I will be using my personal experiences to help you rise above the stigma associated with mental health issues. I invite you to join me on this adventure of self-improvement and success.

Chapter One

Yes, It's Painfully Real

What is anxiety? Do I have it? Many people find themselves wondering about this question. After all, at what point does being anxious cross into becoming a serious issue? Decades of misinformation passed on by mass media has not helped matters. Everyone can fall victim to anxiety; even I was not spared from it.

Perspiration was dripping from my armpits, slowly plunging to my waist as I waited for my eighth-grade schoolteacher to call out my name. Our class assignment was to deliver an oral book report. At least we were allowed to choose the type of book that interested us. That last thought helped me calm my heart down.

However, there was something else throwing my mind into a whirlwind of emotions.

Although the book I had chosen was a fairly straightforward and easy one, there was a hard-to-swallow lump in my throat – as if my heart was stuck there. I detested speaking publicly to a group of any size, strangers or family, prepared or unprepared.

Usually, I was well prepared for all of my assignments. Unfortunately, this one time, rather ashamedly, I did not read the book. I just skimmed through random sections to get a gist of what the author was trying to say, and then developed a simple way to share it with my listeners. At the time, it had seemed like a brilliant idea. Now, I was not so sure anymore.

My original half-baked plan had been to present a "Cliffs Notes" style version of a report, hoping that no one would notice the lack of effort. Perhaps today, one might call it a WikiNotes version report. Now that my name had been called out, beads of sweat immediately appeared on my forehead. My limbs became cramped, and my stomach tied up in a tight knot. My heart was beating erratically, and I was perspiring profusely. I slowly stood up to walk to the front of the class to speak. My voice was shaking as were my hands. I knew all this, and that just made me even more nervous.

When I got to the front of the room, I slowly turned around to face my peers. All eyes stared at me, each pair feeling like a piping hot branding iron. My mouth opened, and words clumsily stuttered out, "When Mrs. Lewis asked us to give an oral book report on any subject that was of great interest to us, I chose Knute Rockne, who became a legendary football player and one of the greatest football coaches in American history…"

Mrs. Lewis immediately interjected and said, "Don, stop right there!"

Oh, no, my heart sank, and I was instantly frozen speechless. *She's found me out,* I thought.

Mrs. Lewis announced, "Class, this is exactly the creativity that I wanted each one of you to follow… to present your report. Don, that's all that I need to hear, you get an A+ for originality. Go take your seat." I exhaled in disbelief and went back to my seat.

As I settled down, I thought, *I have been given a free ticket on this one. I won't be so lucky next time.* The anxiety I experienced that day was extreme. Creating the report, waiting for my name to be called on to present, and then standing up to speak in front of the whole class – all of it had sent me to an extreme level of anxiety. I was a sweaty mess, even after Mrs. Lewis had praised me. This incident always sticks out in my mind whenever I think about me being anxious.

I have a question for you. Has anyone ever told you that your anxiety is not real? That it is not valid? Maybe someone told you, "It's just in your head," and that you are overthinking things. You must have been annoyed at that, right? *Well, yeah, it's in my head. Where else would it be?* Sometimes, as the old saying goes, "It takes one to know one." Some people I have known completely reject the idea of a loved one or a friend having an anxiety disorder. This is very closed-minded of them as far as I am concerned.

When I was a child, and later in my young adult life, it appeared that prolonged anxiety was not taken seriously by most people. Indeed, there was a dearth of research about it compared to what we have today. Moreover, the culture was such that even admitting anxiety was socially unacceptable. Perhaps it was seen by many people as admitting that one had a weakness. Women were seen as being overdramatic, and men were worried about their masculinity being called into question – all of which are illogical reasons.

INDEED, EMOTIONAL AND MENTAL DISORDERS WERE A "HUSH-HUSH" THING WHERE I CAME FROM.

Yes, anxiety is very real. It is a serious issue that needs to be addressed. In this book, I will share how anxiety disorders plagued my life as a child and beat me down. Misery followed me thereafter, like a stalker. Anxiety was always lurking around the corners of my life as a young adult, as well as a mature man with family and business responsibilities. Delving into this is important for you to understand the complex dynamics of anxiety disorders.

What is the Difference Between Stress and Anxiety?

It is vital to understand the difference between stress and anxiety, so we will start there. It is easy to confuse the two. Stress and anxiety are not necessarily unrelated, yet it is essential to understand anxiety as something separate from stress. Hence, before we get to the fun stuff, let us talk about the difference between stress and anxiety.

You and I both experience stress in various ways. You have anxiety at different points of your life, and so do I. I will also take the liberty to say that I do not know a single person that has not been impacted at some level, or in some capacity, by stress and anxiety.

The best way for us to differentiate between stress and anxiety is to think of them as *siblings*. I am the youngest child of four boys in my family, the baby of my large family. The reason I like to associate these two disorders as siblings is that they *share* symptoms. They are interrelated, but not the same. The physical and emotional symptoms are almost too numerous to list; however, there are several things these two relatives share: headaches, tightness in the neck, jaw, and back, loss of sleep, and hypertension.

8

This is not a textbook. Rather, it is a book about the anxiety that I have experienced during my life. So, you and I need to take a look and understand *stress*, after which we will look at *anxiety*. This way, we will be able to extract the two separately from the muddle of their shared symptoms. Let's keep it simple to avoid confusion. The following thoughts can bring about stress:

- *"I have four final exams this week."* Ouch, been there done that.

- *"My house payment is due next Monday, and I don't have all the money to make the payment."* Yikes, I have been in this situation also.

- *"My boss is really angry with me because I forgot to order hamburger buns."* This would be stressful since you serve hamburgers at work this week.

Stress comes upon us from something that happens, outside or externally. It is an external experience and outside-inside force. Stress is very real, and we often do not like the way it makes us feel, even though some stress motivates us to achieve and keep working hard. Conversely, anxiety is quite different. Anxiety can attack us following our reaction to a stressful event. For instance:

- *"I have to take the first of four exams in five minutes."*

- *"I missed my house payment, so I am calling the loan company to try to work out a new payment agreement."*

- *"Since I forgot to order the hamburger buns, I am talking with a bakery to place a rush order on them."*

Anxiety seems to last long after the stress of some outside factor that has been resolved. Sometimes, anxiety continues following a confrontation over the source of the stress. Anxiety comes from within or internally. In that respect, it is an inside-outside experience. Worst of all, anxiety can be like the Energizer Bunny – it just keeps going and going and going, making you feel the after-

9

effects of the stress for a long time. The stress that brought on the anxiety is now over, yet instead of slowly declining, anxiety can be prone to escalating into a severe disorder.

This Is What Anxiety Feels Like

I frequently think, *Why does this have to be me?* or, *Why am I this way?* When I was a boy experiencing anxiety and panic attacks, I recall thinking that all five of my senses were in a war – against some unknown force, as well as each other. Because I have suffered from anxiety as far back as I can remember, I understand what someone enduring anxiety feels.

It is not a fun situation to be in. It can be terrifying and is sometimes debilitating, preventing people from making the most of their lives and talents. That is because anxiety is both a psychological (mind) sensation and a physiological (body) one. What does this mean?

First, Anxiety Is Psychological (Mind)

Severe anxiety affects the mind and reduces your ability to think rationally. As such, it has lasting consequences of victims' personal, social, and professional lives and may include effects such as:

- Inability to concentrate.

- Wanting to panic or escape.

- Thinking the worst is taking place.

- Feelings of there being no escape.

- Fear of what may happen.

- Fear of dying.

- Fear that you are losing control of yourself.

- Fear of choking.

- Fear of smothering.

All these feelings come together to leave the victim borderline dysfunctional. Although effects vary greatly, it is not uncommon for them to worsen over time.

Second, Anxiety Is Physiological (Body)

Anxiety equally and uniformly affects the body. Those who endure severe anxiety know the effect that it has on them physically firsthand. There are serious consequences to your health.

- Shortness of breath.

- Cold sweats.

- Armpits pouring with sweat.

- Pounding heart.

- Chest pain.

- Trembling.

- Dry mouth.

- No saliva to swallow or inability to swallow.

- Hot flashes or chills.

Considering how grave the symptoms are, anxiety is a recognized disorder with different classifications. According to the U.S. Department of Health and Human Services, there are five types of anxiety disorders.

The Five Major Types of Anxiety Disorders

• Generalized Anxiety Disorder (GAD) – Some call this chronic anxiety, which is when someone carries tension, fear, or worry when nothing is provoking it.. GAD can be very complicated because most of life is experienced as anxiety, and it gradually becomes a relatively expected feeling – something that the victim is comfortable with. Our world is easily anxiety-provoking, so a person with GAD tends to have a painful view of life.

• Obsessive-Compulsive Disorder (OCD) – This is when obsessions or compulsions (repetitive behaviors) seem to rule over our common sense. These behaviors can be as simple as repetitive cleaning, washing hands, and constantly rearranging things. All of these only satisfy temporarily, which is why an OCD person must keep on doing them. Anxiety will increase if one attempts to stop the ritual.

• Panic Disorder – This anxiety disorder is represented by often irrational fears that lead to unexpected panic attacks. Symptoms associated with this can be hyperventilation, rapid heartbeats, abdominal pain, dizziness, sweaty hands, and chest pain. These episodes of panic are unexpected and may occasionally repeat themselves.

• Post-Traumatic Stress Disorder (PTSD) – Traumatic events such as military combat, accidents, personal assaults, disasters that were life-threatening, or physical harm can bring about this type of disorder. Certain events that occur long after the original traumatic event can "trigger" PTSD symptoms.

• Social Phobia (or Social Anxiety Disorder) – An overwhelming anxiety of self-consciousness can occur daily in social activities when a person has this disorder.

This phobia can be limited to fears of one certain activity, such as eating in public, talking in public, or public speaking. Otherwise, it can be as severe as just being around people in public anywhere.

> ## ANXIETY IS REAL. PANIC DISORDERS HAVE BEEN SOME OF THE GREATEST CHALLENGES OF MY LIFE.

I still deal with them quite frequently. Overcoming them is a lengthy process, but it is certainly an achievable goal. I habitually find myself saying, "Life gets very lived in" – and brother, that is no joke. We will walk through various situations in this book to help you understand why I say this. I will share with you not just how I have been plagued with anxiety with my own stories, but also how to conquer the anxiety that continues to haunt you.

Anxiety: Friend or Foe?

Asking whether anxiety is your *friend or foe* is almost like asking if money is good or bad. Both anxiety and money need to be respected and controlled. Reducing them to kissing cousins may enhance our ability to grasp them. Over my lifetime, anxiety has been both, my *friend* as well as my *foe*. Anxiety over a paper or a project that is due soon can motivate me to accomplish and succeed in it. In this instance, I would say that anxiety is appropriate, healthy, and has been my *friend*. Whereas anxiety becomes my *foe* when I fail to work through the anxiety properly. I am not beating up on myself. I am simply saying that each of us is responsible for allowing anxiety to take its course with our minds and bodies.

Together, we are going to examine strategies to mobilize ourselves and become adaptive in the middle of an anxiety or panic attack. These are things that you and I can learn from each other. We can win when it appears that anxiety is our foe. We cannot do much about the genetic aspects of the effects of stress, fear, or worry. They are all a big part of anxiety. However, we can learn to be more in control of anxiety when it strikes off-guard.

The Practice of Mindfulness Will Place Anxiety in the Right Perspective

I have always had a fear of public speaking. Little did I know that I would spend most of my life as a public speaker. When I began public speaking as a young man, I spoke about my fear of public speaking to a man I love and admire. This gentleman, Frank Johnson, has been a successful public speaker for the majority of his life. He told me something that I have remembered and embraced repeatedly. He stated, "Don, remember, when you are speaking publicly, no one in your audience is more prepared to speak at the moment, on that subject than you." This taught me a great lesson that I have recalled on so many occasions to help calm my nerves.

Google defines mindfulness as, "A mental state achieved by focusing one's awareness on the present moment, while calmly acknowledging and accepting one's feelings, thoughts, and bodily sensations, used as a therapeutic technique." I have had to learn to shift my awareness to positive things and realize there is really nothing to fear. I tell my mind what to think by keeping it under control. It is vital to our health and success to be mindful of the various ways to manage our anxiety. This is a skill that is fundamental to our contemporary lifestyles so we can keep pace with the dynamics of our modern world.

Tips on Managing Your Anxiety

• Understand the difference between stress and anxiety.

• Accept that what is happening in you is either an outward circumstance (stress) that is occurring to you and that an

14

inward emotion (anxiety) exists when the outward circumstance is no longer a threat.

- Do not try to minimize the stress; admit the emotion.

- Be open and humble – accept your anxiety.

- Learn to participate in your anxiety. Do not try to run. We will discuss how to do this.

- Practice mindfulness.

- Confront the anxiety by breathing slowly and purposely through your nose. Anxiety has its way of making us forget that we need air.

- Be willing to seek help if the emotions continue. Your life matters!

Chapter Two
Kid Stuff

Part One: As a Child

Sweat was beading on my forehead, my arms, and my chest. Dark patches were forming on my clothes around the armpits, collar, and back. Suddenly, I was dizzy, and the air seemed like it had been snatched from my lungs. I began to panic, fear creeping into the back of my mind. From there, everything became progressively worse. "Mama, I can't breathe, I'm dying, I'm dying!" I yelled.

My mother quickly attempted to interrupt my panic attack, encouraging me to breathe slowly, then sit down and calm down. The sound of water running in the bathtub echoed from the bathroom, with a thin layer of what looked like vapor escaping under the bathroom door. Mother had effectively turned the bathroom into a sauna. The steaming hot water had formed clouds of moisture in the air. I noticed the completely fogged wall mirror as my mother led me by my hand into the bathroom. She gestured at me to sit on the edge of the bathtub. I was too shaken to respond, and quietly obliged.

Mother calmly said, "Now breathe slowly, take deep breathes, and make yourself relax." I attempted to follow her instructions for a while, but despite my best efforts, I was unable to get my breathing under control. Mother, not losing her cool for one moment, left me and rushed to the landline to call my physician.

The doctor answered the phone after what felt like a lifetime. She told my mother to bring me to her office, which was located only ten minutes away. Despite that, the drive was terrifying; each minute feeling like it might be my last. This was just one of several panic attacks that I occasionally experienced, usually late at night, during my third and fourth grade in school.

Indeed, I was that young, but still had so many personal issues that were mounting pressure. I was insecure and overweight, and my family was poor. My ears protruded out, and I was also the youngest of four brothers. To add to the pain, I was a left-handed boy, trying to fit into a right-handed world. At school, I was dubbed a slow learner, which to me, translated as, "you are an unintelligent, stupid kid."

My third-grade year of school was what I later recognized as the preview to the living hell of my fourth-grade year. Our family had to move at the beginning of my third-grade year to the other side of town. Leaving my childhood home for an unfamiliar one was jarring for me. I had done reasonably well in first and second grade thanks to the assistance of my sister-in-law. However, everything changed when I became a new student in a new school. It pushed me too far past my comfort zone. This disruptive change consistently threatened me throughout my anxious young life.

Being a big third grader in the new school with new friends as well as living in a different neighborhood certainly brought challenges of its own. One of my newest challenges at school was feeling threatened by my third-grade school teacher, Mrs. Pursee. She wanted to change me and left no stone unturned to that effect. She did not tolerate the fact that I was left-handed. For some bizarre reason, she used to detest it zealously.

She used to constantly remove the pencil from my left hand and place it in my right one. The sound of her sharp voice is still clear in my mind today, "Donald, write right-handed, like a normal person!" Feeling frightened and threatened, I always attempted to write with my right hand, but always to no avail. Please understand that my left-handed penmanship would never win any prize, yet, I could not write anything recognizable with my right hand.

I remember the tension and dread Mrs. Pursee would fill me with as though it was last week. Her mere presence would put me on edge. Eventually, I could not take it anymore and told my mother of my struggle. She, in no uncertain terms, replied that I should write with the hand that God gave me the ability to write with, and if Mrs. Pursee continued to attempt to change me into a right-handed person, she would step in and visit the teacher. This may sound great, but there was a problem. I did not want my mother to get personally involved and create a scene. So, I grudgingly continued to deal with Mrs. Pursee myself. Even though I eventually began having some panic attacks due to her abuse, they were few and far between. They were not severe as yet.

One day, the familiar sound of metal tapping on the linoleum floor began creeping up from behind me. I was anxiously sitting at my desk, awaiting the taunt I knew was coming my way. The sound of Mrs. Pursee's high heels got closer with each tap. At a nerve-wracking gradual pace, the pattering shoes were approaching my desk's right side. I braced myself the best way I knew how, as my anxiety began rising. I knew that at any second now, a three-foot yardstick was going to attack my left hand. Following, Mrs. Pursee would once again force me to change the hand that I was using to write. Obviously, this was abuse.

Somehow, I was the only kid out of twenty-five students or so in our class who was left-handed. This tall, well dressed, bright red-headed stern school teacher was convinced that little Donald was some sort of demon. It was already scary being the new student who knew no one. This abuse just made it worse. I felt as if everyone viewed me as this little monster that was over-weight, freckled-faced, and, God-forbid, left-handed.

That day as the tapping sound approached me, I finally mustered up the courage to stand my ground as a nine-year-old tough guy – following my mother's advice. As predicted, Mrs. Pursee made her sly cat-like approach to my desk and took aim with the big blue yardstick. As she quickly drew her arm back to begin her swat, like she was clobbering an unsuspecting fly, I was ready. As the yardstick was just about to land with all its power on my left penciled hand, I dropped my pencil and caught the yardstick and snatched it from her hands. Then, I stood up and took hold of both ends of the teacher's disciplinary stick.

She looked on in shock as I, with the power of Hercules, broke the stick in half. Oh, the satisfaction and boldness that seemed to consume me at that moment. One might imagine the shock and dismay on the face of my teacher, who I had caught completely by surprise.

With a look of fury coupled with disbelief, she ordered me to take my broken trophy of a stick with me, as she grabbed my arm and promptly made way to the office of our school's principal. With my anxiety creeping up on me again, I was moaning internally as I approached the school's administration office with instructions to see the principal. The administration staff there instructed me to sit down on a couch and wait until the principal arrived. Although I was not showing it outside, I was a wreck and just wanted to go home. No such luck ran my way.

Mr. Marlow, our school principal arrived, and with an exasperated expression, said, "Donald, why did Mrs. Pursee send you to my office?"

With a dry mouth, I squeaked out, "Because I broke her yardstick." Shivering with fear of the wrath I was convinced was going to come, I reached out to the principal and handed him the broken yardstick.

He looked down at the yardstick, then asked, "Why would you break your teacher's yardstick?"

"Because she was trying to hit my hand."

"Donald, why did she try to hit your hand?"

"Because I am left-handed and she keeps trying to persuade me to be right-handed, which is why she hits my left hand. Then she puts the pencil in my right hand, demanding that I start writing right-handed. But I can't!"

An awkward pause followed. I anxiously shuffled my feet, waiting for him to say something. Due to the abuse, I was convinced he would berate me, too. However, with a stricken look on his face, Mr. Marlow calmly instructed, "Donald, return to your classroom immediately and tell Mrs. Pursee to come to my office right now."

"Yes, sir."

Leaving the principal's office without retribution of a lecture or a paddling, a new strength and confidence empowered me. I felt I had been redeemed. I walked into my classroom with my head held high and approached Mrs. Pursee. Fighting the smirk that was emerging on my face, I said, "Mr. Marlow said that he wants to see you immediately." I turned and walked to my desk as I heard the classroom door open and shut. I do not know to this day what Mr. Marlow said to Mrs. Pursee, yet I did figure out two important things:

- First, Mrs. Pursee never struck my hand or chastised me for writing left-handed again.

- Second, it became apparent to me that Mrs. Pursee never really liked me again. Not that she liked me to begin with, but it was different now. She could not do anything about it anymore. The satisfaction that I received from assuming that the teacher got in trouble for swatting my hand is something that I have never forgotten. The only thing that I regret is that I never saw my yardstick trophy again.

I really do not want you to think I am some sort of dinosaur, but many years have passed since a school teacher would even consider trying to change a child's writing hand. Today, hitting a boy or girl in class with a yardstick would guarantee a job dismissal in most schools in America. Indeed, most of the youngest readers must be shocked that this even used to be a practice – that left-handed people were thought of as possessed. Yet, this was the mindset of many "old-school" thinkers.

Help for Slow Learners

Unbeknownst to me, when I was a 10-year-old boy, a psychologist by the name of Samuel A. Kirk was the first person noted to use the phrase, "learning disability," at an educational conference in Chicago, Illinois. The new Association for Children with Learning Disabilities (ACLD) was just being created at the time (1964). Thus, due to this being only recently recognized, the medical profession had not fully assessed and incorporated this information into its practices, much less among educators. The education sector was far from capable of tending to the needs of slow-learners. It was not until 1968 that "hyperkinetic impulse disorder" first appeared in the Diagnostic Statistical Manual (DSM). In 1980, this disorder was renamed Attention Deficit Disorder (ADD).

Of course, back then, because there was insufficient information regarding ADD or my 'disorder,' the school system did not know what to do with me, nor the many other children with various educational challenges.

By the grace of God, I survived third grade with Mrs. Pursee despite our altercations. So, jumping from the frying pan into the fire, I passed into fourth grade. Being a 10-year-old boy, fourth grade was my personal "living hell" of a year. My new teacher was named Mrs. Dryer. She was a tall lady, built with robust shoulders, and was probably nearly 50 years of age. Mrs. Dryer picked up where Mrs. Pursee had left off. It appeared that I was dead meat for her from the start.

In hindsight, I realize I was far from an angel, but I was certainly not the worst. There was no reason for her to instinctively dislike me the way she did. In some way, I had gotten on the bad, bad, side of this teacher. As we started the year, I rapidly got behind in my school work.

I had a horrible time concentrating in class. As I looked at my school work lying on my desk before me, all the words blended together like milk, butter, and sugar dissolving into an indecipherable oatmeal dish. The words on the paper or in the books all jumbled together. I could not think, nor could I focus on my assignments. The smallest of noises made by the students in the classroom distracted me. Things so simple as a student tapping their pencil eraser on the desk, or a girl next to me slightly humming, or a bug slowly crawling down the wall looking for its next meal – it all kept me from focusing where I should be.

Consequently, I did not get school work completed on time. My reading comprehension was horrible. I was kept late in class to catch up on my work, instead of being allowed to go out to recess with the other students. This just made matters worse because the classroom began seeming like a trap to me. I felt like an animal with no freedom in its own cage. Not being allowed to recess also did not help my social situation among my peers.

Finally, Mrs. Dryer had had 'enough' of me and decided the best way to educate me was to segregate me. She placed my desk next to hers at the back of the room against the classroom lockers. My connectivity with the other students was completely disabled, all in an attempt to get me to focus. All this was intensifying my anxiety. One day, when the class went to the school library, I was left in the room with another boy. It was punishment for both of us for not being up-to-date with classroom work. It was after this that serious panic attacks, where I was unable to breathe, began and rapidly became frequent. Concentrating on schoolwork and homework assignments was an almost impossible task for me.

ANXIETY ENCASED ME LIKE AN EGG, SURROUNDED BY AN EGGSHELL.

23

What about this occasion was so severe that it left my mental health in tatters? The boy was named Corky. We sat silently in the class, doing our assignments, while the rest of our classroom and the teacher attended the library. Soon, our school principal used the public address system in our room to speak to Mrs. Dryer to have a female student, who I will call Katie to come to his office. Well, Corky commented on something terribly derogatory about Katie. I decided to remain silent.

When our teacher and students returned to class, Mrs. Dryer called me to her desk and reprimanded me for speaking out negatively about Katie when Mr. Marlow, the principal, called her name. I said, "Mrs. Dryer, that was not me who spoke out, I remained quiet."

She replied, "I know that it was you because Katie has a crush on you, and you don't like her. I know that it was you. Donald, you are lying once again."

Her accusation broke my heart, and I immediately burst into tears. Despite this, or perhaps in spite of this, Mrs. Dryer continued to belittle me and blame me for the incident. I left her desk, walked over to my desk, sat down, and placed my arms on the desk. I laid my head on them and wept for a good while. I was not emotionally well for the remaining part of the day – or the year for that matter.

Things Got Worse

My insecurity, coupled with a horrible school life, kept me anxious and in hopeless misery. I continued having problems with hyperventilating, believing that I was dying, followed by late-night doctor visits and failing academic performance. All of this escalated to a "swallowing disorder." I was unable to swallow anything beyond a fluid substance. I imagined that I was choking when I attempted to swallow food. I would chew and chew and chew until it basically turned into liquid. I would choke to the point that I just knew that I was going to choke to death. The thought of this today churns my stomach.

Thank God for Mother

I was very fortunate that my parents were loving and supportive of me. My mother drove me to school; she took me to the doctor's visits and assisted me in every way possible with my school assignments and reviews for exams. To this end, Mother made several appointments with Mrs. Dryer and visited her. However, her last visit was especially pivotal in getting me the help I desperately needed. I was not there with her, but she later relayed it to me.

Sitting down across from her, my mother said, "Mrs. Dryer, thank you for the time that you have invested in instructing Donald. I'm not sure how much you know already, but Donald is a very sick little boy. He has panic attacks and becomes fearful that he is dying. During the attacks, he is unable to breathe. In the last four months, he has also developed a condition where he chokes on his food and becomes afraid that he is going to choke to death. He becomes ill every morning with the thought of coming to school. He stays worried, knowing that he never pleases you."

After a pause to let what she was saying sink in, she continued, "Mrs. Dryer, I believe that you and I are vital to Donald's health and well-being. His doctor says that he needs many compliments and a lot of encouragement. There are just a few short months left in this school year, but I believe that if you and I work together, we can help Donald turn things around. We can help him to heal emotionally from his issues and salvage his fourth-grade school year. Again, Donald's doctor says that right now, he needs frequent reassurances. Mrs. Dryer, will you work with me on this?"

After a pause to deliberate, Mrs. Dryer responded, "Mrs. Womble, I will do whatever it takes to praise, encourage, and personally assist Donald to help turn things around in his life."

The Unbelievable Happened

I walked into my classroom the day after my mother had the teacher-parent meeting. The first thing I noticed was that my desk was no longer up against the lockers. Mrs. Dryer walked up to me and escorted me to a different desk. This desk was next to the windows, and it was about four seats from the front of the classroom. That day forward, the teacher spent more time with me one-on-one, to make certain that I understood how to do my assignments. There was no frustrated look on her face when I requested help. I was even allowed to go outside for recess with the other students. I finally began to think that the teacher actually might like me.

Miracles Still Happen

The teacher gave the class an art assignment in which she chose half a dozen students' work to exhibit on the class bulletin board. My artwork was among those that were selected, and the teacher publicly recognized it with a huge compliment to me in front of the entire class. My grades soon began to improve. I stopped having panic attacks for the remaining part of the school year, as well as regained the ability to swallow food. Amazingly, I successfully passed the fourth grade and was smoothly promoted to fifth grade.

However, the school was not the only place I faced fears and panic attacks. Almost any time that I was expected to perform in front of a crowd of three or more people, I became extremely anxious, and I would have to fight a panic attack.

Part Two: As a Teen

During ninth grade, a boy and I were caught in a violent fistfight in the biology classroom, just before the tardy bell rang. Admittedly, I was mostly at fault because I had called my classmate "GI-Joe" because this guy made a habit of wearing army fatigues to school. He did not like my comment, so he called my mother a terribly bad name, which was when I stood up and punched him right in the face – bloodying his nose. The fight was on... until our biology teacher stopped us.

He angrily led us by our arms to see the assistant principal. This was still during the stone-age, when corporal punishment by the principal, vice-principal, or coach, was accepted and tolerated in most public schools. School officials could take out the paddle and swat a student on the posterior a few times – or several times, depending on their mood – for even the slightest of misdemeanors. Well, the boy and I both received five paddles on the posterior at the hands of the assistant principal. It was extremely painful.

This same day, at the end of basketball practice, I was in the boy's shower in the gym locker area. A couple of the boys began laughing and making joking remarks about my bruised buttocks. I walked over to a mirror and looked at my rear. I gasped aloud when I saw that my entire backside area was black and blue. Today, there would be a lawsuit for something like this, but not back then. You see, back in those days, most parents supported the decisions of school officials when it came to disciplinary actions for their children. To make matters worse, the boys began shouting, "Womble got licks today, Womble got licks today." Licks were swats with the paddle.

I began to panic as the boys taunted me for my bruises, and I felt a panic attack coming on. I was shaking and unable to breathe. The coach had just retired from the NFL as a professional football player. At the beginning of the academic year, he had threatened all of the male athletes with getting paddled if we were disciplined by the principal for any reason, no matter how insignificant. He had kept his word by paddling several male students already that school year.

As I ran from the shower, soaked with water, I did not take time to dry off. I just feverishly put my clothes on and ran out of the locker room. I was so sore from the principal's whipping that I could not bear the thought of being swatted again. The rest of the week, I tip-toed around this coach.

My panic attacks and anxiety became so disturbing that school year that my physician placed me on a diet of baby food, cream cheese, bread, jelly, and jello, topped with milk and ice cream. This was because once again, I had developed trouble swallowing. The doctor even provided me with a written excuse that allowed me to leave class around mid-morning and mid-afternoon in order to walk to the school cafeteria and eat these little mini-meals, and then return to class. This lasted for a few months. Coincidentally, my basketball coach was also my history teacher, and it was his class that I had to interrupt by leaving to eat one of my mini-meals. I caught a lucky break there.

Anxiety and Panic Attacks Will Not Kill You

I will make this statement several times throughout this book.

> **I THOUGHT THAT I WAS GOING TO DIE, AND EVEN FELT LIKE IT WHEN PANIC ATTACKS STRUCK ME.**

By the grace of God, as well as the support of my parents, family, and teachers, the panic attacks decreased their severity as I got older. I still had anxiety issues and even panic attacks for a long time, yet I learned not to allow them to defeat me from doing things that I wanted to do.

Thus, the panic attacks lessened the older I became. The reality is, I can still have a panic attack. Thankfully, now I know when one is coming and have developed the management tools needed to work through them. Let me share some of these tools with you now.

Tools to Manage Anxiety Disorders' and Panic Attacks

- Yes, receive encouragement. It is imperative that you receive encouragement. Moreover, offer plenty of encouragement if you are supporting an anxious person.

- Breathe purposely and slowly when a panic attack is coming on.

- Take several deep breaths. Just stop… and breathe.

- Realize that you are in control and that your mind is not controlling you.

- Do not fight the panic, just calmly work through it.

- Again, reassure yourself that you will "not die."

- Accept the situation, even when in pain and fear. Look for the positive in every negative.

- Practice the element of boosting your self-esteem.

A Little Bonus on Self-Esteem

How do you Boost Your Self-Esteem?

1. Train yourself to recognize negative thoughts that lead you towards anxiety.

2. Realize that positive thoughts build your inner strength and cast out fears.

3. Talk to yourself. Yes, you read it correctly. Talk out loud to yourself encouragingly.

4. Cope, do not mope – hold your head up high.

5. Believe in yourself, because you were created to function as an individual and excel.

6. Remind yourself that you can, and you will work through panic attacks.

With these basic tools, you will be equipped to manage your anxiety and panic attacks. Of course, these are just a start. They will form the foundation of more complex and effective tools. In the following chapters, I will help you put these tools into various contexts of your life, so you know the best way to manage every situation.

Chapter Three

The Real World

Many discussions and theories typically boil down to one simple question – how will it play out in the "real world?" Alas, we find ourselves at this inevitable juncture as well. What do we even mean by the "real world?" How does it fit into our discussion about anxiety? These are undoubtedly important questions that this chapter will attempt to answer. To that end, let us explore the dynamics of one of the most anxiety-inducing places in our lives: The Work Place.

We will come across a variety of bosses throughout our lives, and what they tell us leaves lasting impacts on our careers.

Boss #1 said, "*You call yourself a leader. Well, your performance today doesn't prove it.*"

Boss #2 said, "*Go make it happen. We will judge by the results.*"

Boss #3 said, "*Here, watch. This is how you do it. Now, let me watch as you do it.*"

Any way you look at it, every boss and every job will carry its own set of emotional anxieties. However, we put up with them because the average person expects to receive two crucial things from their source of employment:

1) A Paycheck

2) Fulfillment

Working at a Young Age

I began working at a very young age. I inherently had an entrepreneurial spirit, even though I did not know the meaning of the word. As an elementary schoolboy, I would dream of ways to work and earn large sums of money – or what seemed large at the time. I realized that I was also attaining a sense of fulfillment from a job well done.

Times were dramatically different back when I was growing up. It was safe in my neighborhood to walk the lawnmower or to knock on peoples' doors to offer my mowing abilities. That was an excellent way to make some money over the summers. I would also walk door-to-door, selling packages of flower seeds. Soon after that, I sold bundles of "All American Greeting" Cards. At eleven years of age, I went to a local, family-owned ice cream shop called Otto's and asked for a job there. Although I was underage, the owner gave me a job sweeping, mopping, and waxing the floor as long as I promised to keep it discreet.

In any case, the chance to work at this ice cream shop was an amazing opportunity in my eyes. Almost every day, the owner of the ice cream shop rewarded me with either a soft drink or an ice cream cone. Not to mention the $8 in cash I received each time I performed my duties.

During my early teen years, I mowed yards and eventually became a stock boy at a local clothing store. That was also a famous national chain of fashion retailers. The store manager paid me in cash, along with a 40% discount on all the clothes I purchased from there. I was excited to have this after school job. It was a dream job for me. I could see myself working up to a floor salesperson when I turned sixteen. Unfortunately, that did not materialize. As we all know, all good things come to an end. My dream job soon became a nightmare. This store went out of business. I was not only disappointed, but my heart also broke because of how abruptly my job was over.

One day, in my depressed state, I felt my dad's newspaper staring at me as it lay on his easy chair – as if it was beckoning me. I picked it up and began thumbing through the papers until I eventually stumbled across the section advertising "local job opportunities." There it was, in black and white: "Newspaper Route Jobs Available."

I dialed the number advertised and inquired about the posting. Soon, a man came to our house and interviewed me. Luckily, he said, "You got the job!" I was so excited. My mother assisted me as we rolled the papers delivered to our home and wrapped rubber bands around them. We would load the papers on the back seat of my mom's car and then take off. I would sit on the passenger side while she drove. As I read the list of newspaper subscribers, I would throw the paper in their yard. This was a six-day per week job – Monday-Friday afternoons and Sunday morning between 2 and 4 am.

This was a cool job for me. Once per month, I walked the route and collected money from paper subscribers. After I had collected enough funds to pay for the papers I distributed, the remaining funds went into my pocket as profit.

I drove myself on the paper delivery after I obtained my drivers' license. With me behind the wheels, I would pay a friend who lived on the next block to assist me with the delivery. This arrangement worked out for both of us. While I was satisfied with what this job offered, I still wanted something that had the potential to pay more.

So after a while, I went to work for a moving company, hauling furniture. After one and half years of being a "helper," as they called it, I was ready to do something that had more of a future for me. By this time, summer had ended, and school classes had commenced. This was serious business because I was the big-time, self-made high school senior on the block.

Distributive Education (DE) was a work program for high school seniors who wanted to work while attending high school. DE Students would go to school for half the day, and work the remaining part of the day on an actual retail job. It was my fortune to find a job as a stock boy for a popular home-grown retail business – a business that you could think of like the lovechild of a Lowes store and a Hobby Lobby. Upon high school graduation, the store's owner offered me the position of "Floor Manager." Excited beyond words, I immediately accepted the position. There had never been anyone as young as me who had held that position before, and that in itself filled me with pride.

Life's giant challenges came for me, and most other people that I know when they hit the real world of adulthood. Just as I continued having anxiety as a child, and throughout adolescence, it overflowed into adult life. My abilities to work through my anxieties grew to where I could function as well as most people. However, the big challenges with an anxious mind became magnified in the adult world.

Adult responsibilities are a wake-up call for most high school graduates. Oh, the challenge of becoming an adult. A person has to learn how to pay for everything in life, such as toothpaste and personal lodging. As we begin taking on more responsibilities, reality sets in, and the pressures of life bombard us.

The Job Pressure

Pressure on the job is relative. Everyone experiences pressure in some form or another, and not all pressure is bad. Some job pressures carry damaging effects on our mental and physical health. Conversely, others give us an incentive to be at the peak of productivity.

Most of us realize that it is common for some form of drama to develop in the workplace. People are people, and each one of us has our personality-related issues. Varying personality traits can create conflict with others we work and live with.

Yes, obviously, stress and conflict on the job have brought intense anxiety to my life – as they have to countless others. At times, I have felt guilty and inadequate at handling my responsibilities. All too often, I have felt less than as an individual. Even more frequently, I have interrogated myself, asking myself numerous questions such as:

"Does anyone know what I'm going through?"

You are not alone. Don't think you are abnormal. According to the ADAA, the Anxiety and Depression Association of America:

- 72 percent of people experiencing stress and anxiety daily say that it does affect them to some degree.

- 40 percent experience excessive anxiety daily.

- 30 percent have taken prescription medication to manage emotional struggles.

- 28 percent admit to having a panic attack or panic attacks.

- 9 percent have an anxiety disorder of some type.

"Am I losing my mind?"

This is a normal thought that I have had many times ever since I was a boy. Don't miss this; you should address it immediately. Your brain is not breaking down, nor is anxiety itself a mental illness. Don't tell yourself that you are going mad because anxiety and panic attacks do not kill people. Fear is overwhelming you, but tell yourself that you are safe.

"When will I have another attack?"

I have never had to concentrate about having another panic attack. This is because when you do this, you may work yourself into a frenzy of some sort. You are capable of working through panic attacks, and we will discuss this later in the book.

"Will I ever overcome this anxiety or these panic attacks?"

Please don't lose hope.

YOU CAN GAIN CONTROL AND YOU CAN LEARN TO HEAD OFF PANIC ATTACKS BEFORE THEY EMERGE.

You and I may deal with anxiety issues for the rest of our lives, but we can at least learn tools to cope with them. There is a great reward as we learn how to deal with them and defeat them. Anxiety in life will always be present to some degree. We can train ourselves to become prepared to control our anxiety disorders.

The Main Perpetrators of Work-Related Stress

Perpetrators have no fear, and they come in all shapes and sizes of stress on the job.

LEARN TO IDENTIFY YOUR STRESSORS.

Do not run from them or avoid them. Rather, learn to understand how to meet them head-on and work through them. The ADAA gives the following as the main culprits of job-related stressors:

- Dealing with problems (49 percent)

- Interpersonal relationships (53 percent)

- Deadlines (55 percent)

- Staff management (50 percent)

However, there are other job stressors out there, such as:

- Trauma

- Lack of support

- Lack of communication from the top

- Management or supervisor change

- Role conflict

- Long hours

- Job insecurity

- Over-supervision (micro-management)

- Few opportunities for promotion

• Discrimination

• Harassment

Learning Ways to Manage Anxiety on the Job

The Anxiety and Depression Association of America answers some excellent questions that help us understand how we can cope with our anxiety. All too often, people deal with anxiety in an unhealthy manner.

• How do men deal with job anxiety?

Men are more likely to use *illicit drugs* and have sex more frequently than women.

• How do women deal with job anxiety?

Women are prone to *eat more* and talk to friends and family to cope with job-related stress.

To manage job anxiety, I want to list some healthy ways that any of us can embrace and put to practice. This is not rocket science.

1. *Ask someone for some help.* It's okay to admit you do not understand something. This may take some vulnerability on your part, but it will pay off.

2. *Try to get reasonable deadlines.* Not all deadlines are reasonable, but attempt to find some compromise. Be honest and up-front.

3. *Have good relationships with co-workers.* Learn people's names and call them by them. Most of us like hearing others repeat our names. Try this by reading the name tag of the store cashier or the salesperson, and then call them

by name. Say, "Thank you, Jennifer." Watch Jennifer's response when you speak her name – you'll see the difference for yourself.

4. *Don't get mixed up in gossip at work (or anywhere). "What goes around, comes around"* is a timeless proverb. Gossip will come back and bite us, and it will be bloody. So it is best not to partake in it altogether.

5. *Encourage co-workers and your supervisors.* When I was a young man, an older gentleman taught me the law of reciprocity. What you and I "give-out," it will someday "come back to us." Thus, encourage and appreciate people if you want the same for yourself.

6. *Be helpful.* Each of us will benefit when we are helpful to those that we work with. Trade a day off with someone or loan some lunch money to them if they left their wallet at home (likely excuse, right). Be caring and loving, but don't allow people to run over you. Be cautious, but exercise your generosity.

You may agree it's best to use wisdom when dealing with the boss and work associates. I agree with the approach that I heard of when one woman was being questioned by her boss. It went something like this: "When my boss asked me who is the stupid one, him or me, I told him everyone knows he doesn't hire stupid people." That is a smart woman!

New Job – New Challenges

Let me challenge you if you are continuing your career with a job or if you are starting a new career. I moved from a career where I had worked in one place for over 25 years in November 2006. I left security, great pay, and familiarity as I entered into a completely new line of work.

Earlier in 2006, I earned a master's in business administration (MBA). That same year, I became an insurance salesman. By the end of 2007, I began working as a project manager for a friend. I went from one high-stress job to another high-stress job within a span of days. As most of us would agree, every old or new job has new challenges. This one was no different. Some of the new challenges consisted of:

- Computer and software abilities

- Team dynamics

- Performance demands

- Organization structure

- Required skills

- Business's language

- Company culture

- Work overload

- Success and failure

Believe me, I had my fears and doubts. I carried along with me the anxiety disorder that has hovered over me – that too in its own special made backpack. Indeed, there were countless days where I thought:

- "Dear God, what have I done?"

- "Will I ever get the hang of this new position?"

- "Am I going to get fired over this dumb decision?"

- "This is not in my gifts and abilities category."

• "I miss doing something I was familiar with for many years."

All these thoughts are normal, and they can even be healthy. Don't give up. Keep learning and applying yourself. You will learn how to handle the new pressures along with the new and old anxieties. Anxiety will always be near or in the workplace.

However, that does not mean you need to give into it. You can defeat your anxiety by trying these tactics:

1. Improve your *attitude.*

2. *Encourage* others.

3. *Communicate* with others.

4. *Stay out* of the way of *gossip.*

5. Keep *good relationships.*

6. *Work* with *deadlines* that the entire office, warehouse, or shop can benefit from.

Use your anxiety to grow and develop as a person. Don't run and don't complain about work anxiety. Become a better person by working through it. Believe in yourself. You CAN do this!

Chapter Four

Love and Marriage

My wife and I began our relationship very young – at least by today's standards. Kathy and I began dating when I was sixteen, and she was seventeen. I always went for older women. Please don't tell her I said that! At the end of my sophomore year of high school, I gave Kathy a promise ring that was actually a small wedding band. We frequently discussed marriage, along with dreams that each of us had in life. We even went to Zale's and picked out wedding rings that I placed on layaway.

At the end of my junior year of high school, which was Kathy's senior year, I had our rings paid off, and I picked them up out of layaway. Kathy was unaware of my financial feat, and she was unaware that I was ready to pop the big question. I felt that since Kathy was graduating from high school, I had to secure the deal as soon as possible so I would not lose her to someone else.

Kathy and I enjoyed doing many simple things when we dated. We would frequent an old city park in a nice part of our hometown of Midland, Texas. We enjoyed walking around just about any park as we held hands and discussed our future with anticipation. However, that old park was our favorite.

This particular Friday night, we drove up to that old park. I opened the door, got out, and held the door open for her as well. I stepped to the side of the car, and the conversation went like this:

As I got down on my knees before her and presented the engagement ring, I asked, "Kathy, will you marry me? Will you be my bride?"

With a look of pure joy on her face, Kathy replied enthusiastically, "Yes, you know that I will."

It was that simple! We laughed, immediately overwhelmed with happiness. I stood up, and we kissed a few times. I quickly slid the engagement ring onto her finger, kissing her once more. Then, we held hands as we walked around the park for a while, discussing how we would proceed from here.

The next year, two months following my high school graduation, we got married. That was in August of 1972. Yes, we are still married. If I can hurry and complete the book, we should stay married awhile longer. I sure hope so anyway.

Me – the Anxious Spouse

Well, I must confess that my wife, Kathy, married the anxious spouse. A saving grace of our relationship for these many years is that we are one another's best friend. We enjoy being together more than with anyone else. All relationships struggle, and our relationship has not been any different.

At the same time, despite my anxiety, it has been to our advantage that I am a self-motivated person. No one has to drag me out of bed, nor do I need anyone coaching me to get busy or stay busy. If anything, I have needed a coach to inspire me to slow down, rest, and take more time off.

Throughout our marriage, I have dealt with my anxiety disorder more times than I can count. My wife was always present to lend me her support and encourage me through vulnerable times. One particular anxious phase in my life occurred some years ago. Our daughter was in her early teens, our youngest son was in his late teens, and our oldest son lived away from home. This combined to create a concoction that gave me severe anxiety.

This turbulent whirlwind lasted approximately five years. I will share more on this period and its anxiety and depression in the following few chapters. Severe anxiety will find its shape under the right circumstances, and it will affect all the pressure points of our lives.

> *Over 40 million adults in the United States suffer from some form of anxiety disorders. That means that 18% of the population agonizes from these conditions.* ~Anxiety and Depression Association of America (ADAA)

If an anxiety disorder has merged with your marriage, understand that you are not alone. Anxiety disorders are the most common form of emotional illness.

Recognize Common Symptoms of Anxiety

Before we discuss some of the symptoms of anxiety, there a few important things that need to be said. Any anxious person should remind themselves of the things that bring anxiety to them. Situational anxiety is common to most people when stressful situations arise. The following signs of severe anxiety disorders are usually diagnosed over a period of six to eight months. These may flow from one extreme to the other, and can include:

Fatigue

Insomnia or Excessive Sleeping

Overeating or a Loss of Appetite

Irritability

Lack of Humor, Smiling or Laughing

Crying or the Inability to Shed a Tear

Pain or Stiffness

Lack of a Sex Drive

Sweating

Shallowness of Breath

Lack of Concentration

Fear of Doom

Excessive Worry

Trembling

Unwanted Thoughts

Encourage Your Spouse to Seek Medical Attention

Encourage your spouse to search for adequate medical attention when any symptoms of anxiety arise and linger. My wife has always been my cheerleader. She closely observed me and acted the moment she sensed anxiety originating from me. If it was not within her means to do something about it, she would always give me a gentle nudge to see my doctor.

> **UNTREATED ANXIETY CAN DESTROY YOUR MARRIAGE, YOUR FAMILY, AND YOUR LIFE.**

I am more than thankful and grateful to my wife for her consistent support over the decades. She has been endlessly loving and patient. Her opinions have mattered and encouraged me in the most troublesome of times.

In Sickness and in Health

While having fun with the family, I injured my back.

My wife, our two boys and I were visiting family in Midland, Texas. We decided to take a day out and go to play on the sandhills in Monahan's with the boys, which was about fifty miles away. Most people have never heard of the Monahan's Sandhills State Park in Monahan's, Texas, despite how extraordinary it is. It looks like a piece of the Sahara Desert in the United States.

I was in my mid-thirties, full of "vim and vigor." I thought I was up to a day of fun. We took a board that I made in my seventh-grade shop class, about thirty inches long and one foot wide. Formica was glued to the bottom. I had designed it for sliding on the sand dunes. The goal of playing in the sandhills was to sit on the board and slide down the sand dunes. To ensure the journey downhill was smooth and safe, I would slick up the bottom of the board with a piece of paraffin wax. It was a scorching hot day, and it didn't take long for us to tire out.

Imagine sliding down the sand, then climbing up to the top to do the whole thing over again. Our youngest son was about three years old at the time. This little man got tired, so I started carrying him on one arm and the board in the other. On one trip up the sand hill, I was struggling to get to the crest. Suddenly, I felt and heard something pop. I didn't realize what had happened at the time but later realized that I herniated a disc in my lower back.

It's an odd thing when that happens. A person may not have immediate back pain. Rather, the left or right leg will abruptly start hurting. Once the pain emerges, it will grow to sharp leg pains, up and down the leg. My leg pain settled in my left leg. I later learned that the herniated disc in my back was pressing against the sciatic nerve, which is why the leg pain was so severe. We finished out our day and drove back to Midland.

I thought I had merely pulled a muscle in my leg. I tried countless things to relieve the pain until it became almost unbearable. Since I am a genius (that's a joke), I finally realized I had a very serious problem on my hands. I wrestled with sleeping every night, the excruciating pain forcing me into an insomniac.

Each morning, I crawled out of bed, unable to stand. On my hands and knees, I struggled to get to the restroom. I desperately held onto the commode to pull myself up. Then, I battled to carefully enter the shower, writhing in pain. It took me a while to be able to place any weight on my left leg at all. Everything became a painful chore – a painful blur. Following the shower, I slowly dressed then hopped around the house. I would endure the discomfort until I maneuvered to my car, which would restart the moment I got out of the car at my destination.

My daily routine at the time was quite hectic. At 6 am I made my way to teach a class in a Bible College in Fort Worth, Texas. I stood and taught the class for one hour and fifteen minutes. Then I drove to my office to carry out my responsibilities for the rest of the day and evening. I did all this constantly in pain – not relenting for a second.

My wife encouraged me to see our doctor for several months. I was hard-headed, thinking that it would eventually work itself out. Finally, I submitted to my wife's recommendation and went to the doctor. He examined me and set up an MRI (Magnetic Resonance Image). The MRI revealed that a disc in my back had herniated. My family practitioner sent me to a physical therapist who worked on my back to strengthen it. Over time, the pain began to reduce and became manageable. A couple of months later, I went into surgery for a Laminectomy, which involves the trimming of the disc in the back or neck that had herniated.

This whole process lasted a grueling eight months. It encouraged my anxiety and depression that lasted for some time – even after the issue had been resolved. Faith in God, my wife's encouragement, talented doctors, along with my tenacity to not quit, pulled me through this testing time.

A Caring Spouse Maintains Your Sanity

Seek professional counsel for encouragement and guidance the moment you feel like you need it. Dealing with an anxious spouse is tiring and challenging. While they will willingly lend you their support, you need to avoid being a burden on them, as well as that alone may trigger anxiety and depression within them.

Conversely, if you are on the other end, i.e., your spouse is struggling with anxiety or depression, then here are a few simple suggestions. To stay loving and to keep your sanity, remember to:

Understand that it is not your fault.

Accept the fact that your life's love has an anxiety disorder.

Keep your head clear; do not run.

Use extreme caution when discussing personal issues with someone of the opposite sex. A professional counselor or medical care professional is an exception to that rule. In weak moments, even good people can become tempted.

You cannot play God. It is not your obligation to fix your spouse.

Admit to it when you feel frustrated with the situation you find yourself in. Honesty is vital.

Words from the Anxious One

As the anxious one in our marriage, I carry a huge responsibility to work hard on our relationship. I am blessed to have a loving, faithful, and strong spouse. She has walked by my side and remained supportive of me through the roughest of times. I often refer to the challenging period as "the time that I lost my mind." Now, I realize that I did not lose my mind. It is still intact. I wondered off into severe anxiety, and I had a terrible time crawling out of that horrible pit.

To maintain a strong, healthy and vibrant marriage, there are key relationship components that need to adhere. While I admittedly do not know everything, I do know situations vary couple to couple. Let me share some key essentials that I have learned, by dealing with anxiety in marriage.

Key Essentials to Manage Anxiety

1. Get professional help if you display consistent anxiety symptoms.

2. Humble yourself and admit that you have a disorder.

3. Don't be stupid and stubborn.

4. Admit your faults. Yes, confess them.

5. Find humor in situations, and learn to laugh at yourself.

6. Talk it out – COMMUNICATE.

7. Accept support from your spouse.

8. Believe and trust.

9. Remember the emotional, physical, and spiritual needs of your spouse.

10. Socialize.

11. Reach out to others who may be going through similar anxieties.

When I get my mind off my problems and help someone else, it is fulfilling and brings inner healing to me. Through all the pain and confusion, you can, and you will grow together. Anxiety may not be gone altogether, but you will have it under control by working on it over time. Together, you can face anything. Stay loving, supportive, and faithful to the commitments you have made to one another. Do not let something like this undermine the special bond you share.

Chapter Five

Bad Decision(s)

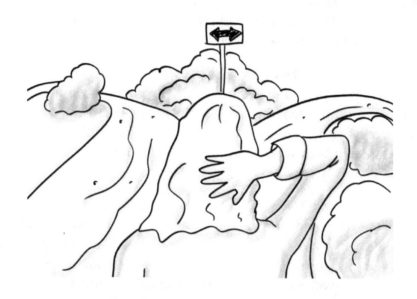

Bad Decision #1 – Exposed My Anxiety

My phone rang, so I answered it, and the ensuing brief conversation went like this:

Me: "Hello."

My 15-year-old son: "Dad, you and Mom have to get home immediately. We destroyed our neighbors' swimming pool."

Me: "Unplug the pump."

My 15-year-old son: "IT'S TOO LATE!"

We ended that call, and as I left my office, I called my wife. She said she would meet me at our house. We both pulled up in front of our house at the same time. We parked our cars and walked down the street to our neighbor, who lived near the far east corner of our fence. We approached our neighbors' house, and the lady of the house was standing in the front yard. As soon as she saw us, she began telling us what had happened. She was crying as she was trying to tell us that we had destroyed their swimming pool.

Slowly, we walked around the corner of their house toward their back yard. Massive chunks of their gunite swimming pool were protruding from the ground. The diving board was almost in a perfectly vertical position, "shooting up" towards the sky. As we stood in their back yard, our mouths dropped wide open, and our eyes filled with tears.

My wife and I were in utter shock and dismay. For a few minutes, we could not handle what we were seeing, let alone speak. Then, almost in unison, the words painfully escaped our lips, "Oh my gosh, I am so very sorry. I don't know what to say other than I (we) are so sorry and saddened by this." I went on to add, "I don't how, but we will make this right with you."

Looking back at this tragedy, I can still see this dear lady standing next to the disaster site, stricken with shock and dismay. Her voice was trembling, and she was unable to collect herself. She began telling us:

The Lady: "Every year around the same time, as you drain your pool, the water flows into our yard. In the past, we received it as a great way to water our yard for a couple of days. Normally, our pool is full of water, so the extra water in the yard that comes from your pool has never disturbed us. But this year, we decided to do some re-tile work on the pool, so we drained the pool of water."

Me: "We were unaware that draining our pool each year was an issue. We live on a one-acre tract, and so as we drain our pool, we rotate the drainage hose back and forth across our acre. This is our fault, and we don't have the words to say to show our sorrow. I know that I've already said this, but we will make this right with you."

Bad, Stupid Decision

This gunite pool was empty. Buried in the ground, it began to float out of its original spot. The pool lifted out of the ground, yet not in a whole piece. It looked like an earthquake occurred. Visualize a 50,000-gallon swimming pool, along with the in-ground plumbing pipes, protruding out of the ground in chunks and pieces. To top it off, this family had two teenagers that had their swimming pool demolished forever. In hindsight, if I had drained our pool correctly, this would not have happened. I made a bad, stupid decision!

Can someone say, *"ANXIETY?"*

I was currently battling my anxiety-related disorder. Recent events in our lives, and this bad decision brought my wife and me to a raised level of anxiety. Simultaneously, this elevated-anxiety brought us to an emotional low. I contacted our home owner's insurance company and explained the dilemma to our agent. The insurance agent reviewed our policy, called us back, and explained, "Mr. Womble, I am uncertain that your policy has a contingency to pay for this event. I will contact the home office and ask them for a review and give you their response in a few days. Be aware that there is a probability this policy does not cover you."

I wanted to disappear somehow. Maybe you have seen some of the Southwest Airlines commercials. In these commercials, someone does something that brings them ultimate embarrassment. The narrator says, "Wanna get away?" Absolutely,

I wanted to get away. I wanted a one-way ticket to anywhere where I could stay forever. Deep down inside, my wife may have been wishing for the same thing – not for herself, but rather for me. For a couple of weeks, I was the most unpopular person on our block and in our house.

ANXIETY CARRIES THE WEIGHT AFTER THE STRESSFUL EVENT HAS PASSED

I dug into the filing cabinet and located our home owner's insurance policy. I read and then re-read the entire document. There was one clause that appeared to contain the answer to our predicament. Nonetheless, I was still waiting for a call from our insurance agent.

Due to this, my wife and I discussed our options if the insurance company refused to take care of our neighbors' destroyed swimming pool. This was becoming more serious as the days went by. We decided to be transparent with our two teens. We wanted them to know the severity of the situation.

I called a family meeting, and the four of us sat down in the living room. I told our family that if the insurance does not pay to remove our neighbors' pool's debris and replace their pool, then we will have to find another way of resolving this problem. We were ultimately responsible for the disaster, and we may have to sell our house and use the home equity to repay our neighbors for my negligence.

Our children were solemn yet mature; they supported whatever had to happen. I wish to highlight the things that each one us can learn from this poor decision and bad experience. Even when you and I are emotionally stressed and full of anxiety, we must always act with integrity.

Good News Helps Relieve Anxiety

A few days later, our insurance agent contacted me. Our policy covered this unfortunate event. The insurance adjuster visited our neighbors, and they eventually came to an agreement on the claim. In a few weeks, our neighbors received a check to pay for everything they needed. Needless to say, the Hallelujah chorus rang out in our heads for a good, long while.

Ultimately, our neighbors chose not to use the funds that our insurance company provided for them to remove the cratered pool and replace it. Bad news travels rapidly. All of our neighbors knew of the pool's destruction and that I was the responsible party. Yet, they did not know that the family was properly reimbursed for their pool's destruction. The demolished swimming pool stayed in its disarrayed state for many years. It was extremely painful to drive by and glance over and see the wrecked pool. A portion of the pool was in plain sight, from the street, leaving a visible reminder to all of its sad fate.

Bad Decision #2 – Intensified My Anxiety

Remember my herniated disc, as well as my back surgery from the previous chapter? Well, there is more to the story. The next year, I herniated another disc in my back while playing basketball with some friends. I was back to the routine of struggling to walk without limping. My physical therapist taught me various exercises and positions to strengthen my back muscles. These exercises also served as useful techniques to manage the pain and promote healing without going back to surgery.

Despite the physical challenges, the main battle I faced was my anxiety. I could not stop my regular schedule, and so the doctor prescribed muscle relaxers. The muscle relaxers may have relaxed my back muscles, yet they did not allow me to relax mentally. They prevented me from sleeping. One day, when I had a sleepless night, I went to the pharmacy to pick up a muscle relaxer refill.

Driving home, I gradually became increasingly frustrated with the whole situation. My messed up back, my leg pain, the pills keeping me awake, and the $45 that I had to spend at the pharmacy – all added to my dilemma. On top of all this, trying to work and provide for my family while in continuous pain was extremely agonizing. I arrived at the house and was getting more anxious and angrier with each passing second.

I pulled into our driveway, stopped the car, opened the door, and stepped out. My irritation had mounted. I took the bottle of pills and threw them into the yard. As luck would have it, the bottle slammed into a tree in our yard, and of course, the plastic shattered. All the pills scattered over the yard in a 10-foot radius. I said, "Well, that's just great" (or something along those lines). I proceeded into the garage and became stricken with guilt. I was guilty of losing my temper and for wasting the money on the pills.

I walked in the direction of the tree and stooped down to crawl on the grass to begin picking up the pills, one at a time. To make matters worse, somehow, my dog got out of the house and began running all around the yard and in the street. Here I am on my knees in pain, yelling at my dog to come back. Guess who pulled up next to the curb by my house while I was in the midst of this ridiculous moment? Well, of course, the humane society truck. The "dog catcher," as I call him. He got out of the truck and approached me while I am on my knees in the yard, looking like an absolute mess. He proceeded to say:

Dog Catcher: "Sir, your dog is loose and does not have on a collar with its tags."

Me: "Yes, sir, I am sorry. As you can see, I am in a precarious situation. My back is injured, and I am picking up my prescription of pills that I accidentally spilled (a little lie). So while I was here

56

on my knees, picking up the pills, somehow, my dog got out of the house."

Dog Catcher: "Well, it doesn't matter how it happened. I am writing you a citation for your dog not having valid dog tag registrations."

Me: "Well, that's really kind of you. I appreciate your sympathy and your cheerfulness to write a citation to a man in my situation. Since you're so good at it, why don't you write me up twice?"

Dog Catcher: "I will write you up twice. One for the dog and the other for the attitude to resist the citation."

Me: "Resist the citation? You're an idiot!"

Dog Catcher: "Do you want three?"

Me: "Bring it on…"

Well, you might say, that didn't go too well, did it? The anxiety, the pain, and the depression had me in a vulnerable frame of mind. One bad decision led to another and another and another. I try not to blame the bad decisions on my mental condition because I am responsible for the decisions that I make. However, it is important to acknowledge them as a factor.

> Let's Learn from This: Remember to respond with integrity when a bad decision creates a bad experience.
>
> Do not take short cuts if there is any chance of harming someone or someone else's property.
>
> Get all the facts when bad things happen; assume nothing.
>
> Be humble and admit when you are wrong, especially to the person that you wronged.
>
> Apologize to the person(s) for your offense.

Purpose to replace or make things right when you have wronged someone.

Do the necessary research to find the right answers.

Count the cost of your dilemma.

Look at all honorable options.

Involve your spouse in the decision-making process.

Communicate with your family. I have discovered that when we hide too much from our children, it can come back to haunt us later.

Make this a teachable moment for your loved ones.

Pray, if you believe that God is your father and that He is in control of your life.

Inform your family of the conclusion to the challenge.

Rejoice in the victories.

Always do the right thing.

Do not lose your temper.

Do not throw your bottle of prescription pills.

Do not make your city dog catcher angry.

Learn from your mistakes.

This is a simple depiction of so many things in our lives. Even though our decision may not be inherently wrong, there are many scars left, remaining to be seen for a long period. Let us learn from our mistakes and grow to do things better next time!

Chapter Six

I've Got a Secret

I had a *secret,* one that would have far-reaching consequences if leaked. As the leader of a few thousand people, I was utterly afraid, humiliated, and emotionally messed up. In the spirit of honesty, I should disclose that there is something else that I have *not* mentioned in this writing. The truth is, I was the lead pastor of one of the largest and fastest-growing churches in the city where I lived. Moreover, I was responsible for being a husband, father, grandfather, and leader of a large staff.

As I mentioned earlier, I was in a messed-up frame of mind. I did something that I personally never thought I would be capable of doing. I made a telephone call to a psychiatrist in Fort Worth, Texas, to arrange an appointment for *myself*. This psychiatrist was highly recommended and respected, so I decided to take the big plunge.

I walked around for some time, thinking, *"I've got a secret."* Well, I actually had many secrets at the time. Please understand that I had been a leader in my community for about twenty-five years. I had so many massive secrets hiding away inside me. Fortunately, I was not involved in anything that was categorically illegal, unethical, or immoral. Yet, I had embarrassing secrets nonetheless. Some of the secrets were:

- I was *psychologically* drained.

- I wanted to *run* away.

- I was *fearful* of failure.

- I was *paranoid*.

- I was *exhausted*.

- I was *ashamed*.

- I suffered from prolonged *anxiety*.

- I was *depressed*.

- I was *afraid* people would find out.

I do not want this chapter to be about me. Allow me to address some of the things that I experienced that may resonate with you because of something that you went through at some time in your life. In order to experience personal growth, each of us must be humble enough to admit where we are in our lives. I was carrying the mental load of far too many "secrets" over my head, and they weighed me down. All too often, I pondered, "What if people found out?" "What would they think about me?" "I could get fired," and "I will lose others' respect." This was a very challenging predicament that I had found myself in. I did not know how to continue with the way things were going in my life.

Dark Days

I went for counseling with the psychiatrist for over three years. After a few visits, he decided to prescribe me an anti-depressant to take. I began consuming 10 mg per day, and before I worked my way off of the medication, I was taking 120 mg of the prescription daily.

When a person is a leader, and constantly in the public eye, personal relationships become few and far between. It is easy not to want to allow people into the inner circle of one's personal life. Everyone experiences bad days, but then there are those that I would categorize as *dark days*.

THE DOOR TO PERSONAL GROWTH IS ALWAYS OPEN WHEN A PERSON COMES TO GRIP WITH THEIR CONDITION.

It is most difficult to be vulnerable and say, "I can't live this way any longer. I will accept whatever comes my way."

The Fear of Rejection

I had a fear of rejection. To be honest, the fear of rejection will make any one of us anxious. This fear manipulated my anxiety. I was a pastor – a leader in the community for many years. People had their expectations of who I was supposed to be. People look at a leader and begin to picture what someone in that position should be like and should *look* like.

It is honestly amusing to me when I look at the expression of someone when they find out that I am a pastor of a church. Almost immediately, an invisible wall goes up, and it seems like I have been branded in some negative way. I am fine with this. I honestly think it is hilarious. The thing about it that I do not like is when this wall prevents me from having the opportunity of a healthy relationship with this person.

I have been the pastor of two different mid-size churches in the same area for over thirty-five years. Sometimes, I will meet someone, and they will tell me, "Aren't you a church pastor?" I sometimes humorously reply, "Yes, but not enough to hurt." Immediately, I will get a response from the person with a laugh, or a questioning or puzzled look. I do this to break the ice. I am just like most normal individuals. I do not like rejection, and I sometimes fear rejection.

Lessons we can learn from the fear of rejection:

- Be you! You have to be genuine.

- Be who you are, and if others are not pleased, they are the ones who have "a problem." It is not your problem.

- Rejection does not define you.

- Rejection has nothing to do with you being a bad person.

- Determine accepting rejection by accepting yourself. There is not one person in the world that has not suffered rejection in some way and by someone.

Sensitive Person, Own up to It

The majority of my life, I have not dealt with criticism very well. I have always battled not to take criticism personally. When I went through five years of emotional turmoil, something extraordinary happened. I came out of it not only more accepting of myself and more accepting of others, but also with a greater concern for people in pain. I matured as an individual, and I was in my mid-fifties. Indeed, who said, "You can't teach an old dog new tricks."

Being highly sensitive breeds anxiety. In many ways, I have been highly sensitive for the majority of my life. Doing what I do in life, one would think that I had "thicker skin." My skin is not as thick as I had wished, nor as thick as this book may make it appear.

> **IF YOU ARE A "SENSITIVE PERSON," LEARN TO BE RESILIENT TO CRITICISM. IT IS IN YOUR BEST INTEREST.**

How can you determine if you are a sensitive person?

Do you:

- Get your feelings hurt easily?

- Process things too deeply?

- Read too much into what people say about you or the way that they look at you?

- Have a difficult time being who you really are in public?

- Become irritated by certain noises? People have some background music and different noise peculiarities.

- Overreact and become defensive and feel threatened?

People who have some of these characteristics may not necessarily be "anxious." Conversely, anxiety is very possible when people with anxiety disorders are placed in sensitive situations.

Lessons we can learn from our sensitivity:

• Acknowledge and admit that you are sensitive – Own it!

• Acknowledge and admit that your sensitivity is robbing you of your inner peace.

• Acknowledge and admit that your sensitivity inhibits you from being real.

• Begin to apply some things to get some "thick skin."

Learning to be a thick-skinned person:

• Become aware of the things that offend you. Stop over-reacting.

• Stop exaggerating or over-thinking what was said to you.

• Believe in who you are as a person. Don't seek everyone's approval.

• Step outside of your comfort zone from time to time. It will make you more tolerant of others or things that you do not normally like.

• Purposely request some constructive criticism from others. This requires you becoming vulnerable.

Control Your Mind, Don't Let It Control You!

Anything controlling us; breeds anxiety inside of us.. You and I have an innate, inborn ability to control our thinking rather than our thinking controlling us. We are fully capable of taking control of our thought processes as long as we apply ourselves to that end. Let me illustrate this.

Your cell phone rings, and you look at the caller ID. The caller ID reveals that it is your boss or supervisor making the call. Be honest, what is your first thought? Some of us would think, "Oh, no, I wonder what in the world has gone wrong. I'm in trouble. He/she never calls me unless I've messed up on something." Finally, you get the courage to answer the phone call.

You hit the answer button, and your boss says, "I have two extra tickets to a Dallas Cowboys football game for this coming Saturday. I just wanted to check and see if you would like to have them." You pause for a moment in dismay, momentarily amazed by what you have just heard. Then you respond, "I would love to have those tickets. I've been wanting to go to a Dallas Cowboys game this season, but the opportunity had not surfaced before now. Thank you so much!"

Come on, confess it. Your mind was trying to control you into thinking that the worst possible thing is happening at work. The majority of us are conditioned to think the worst for given situations. "Your mind thinks the worst! My mind thinks the worst!" Don't beat yourself up over it, and just recognize it.

"LEARN TO RECOGNIZE THAT YOUR MIND THINKS THE WORST."

Suffering Heavy Anxiety as a Leader

In the first chapter, we discussed *stress*. Stress is the reaction to *external* experiences that places us under emotional pressure. Stress can creep up on us from anything that we deem important. It might be a meeting or a deadline at work. Alternatively, maybe it is to get the garbage out to the street before the sanitation truck arrives.

I had been leading a church for 25 years as the lead pastor. Understand that a church is made up of people. The church building is just the vehicle that is used for "the people" to meet, be taught, and enjoy good fellowship. The real mission of the church is outside of the four walls of the church building. Because the church *is people*, recognize that people are human beings. If you and I will be honest about this, we will admit that each of us is imperfect, flawed, and messed up mortals.

I know some great people who have horrible interpersonal skills. Truthfully, too many of us do not mature, and as a result, we fail miserably in our relationships. Why? Because we are selfish instead of selfless. We need to learn to empathize with others and extend help to them.

Every organization contains people. These may be any organization such as a church, a business, a school, a college, a partnership, or even a sports team. People are people, and too often, people are on the look-out for becoming number one. Thus, here are some of the *external stresses* that have worn on me for over many years:

- Gossip

- Criticism

- Expectations

- Negativity

- Finances

- Judgmentalism

- Infidelity

- Apathy

- Staff Issues

- Feeling Overwhelmed

Being a leader can be extremely stressful. Someone has said, *"Everything rises and falls on leadership."* I believe this statement. Often times, things occur in an organization, and the leader has little control to prevent it. Leadership is always challenging. It can be much like trying to put a puzzle back together again at times. When some of the puzzle pieces have been destroyed or damaged, things seldom go back to normal. It is still the leadership's responsibility to lead the organization toward success. And remember, you never reach success – you are always striving for it, no matter how wealthy, accomplished, or influential you are.

After the *stress* of the *external event, anxiety* can live within us. The external turns in to an internal condition. Anxiety disorders can easily emerge inside of us without us even realizing them at first. When anxiety surfaces, learn the tools that work best for you to manage them. Practice these tools to make sure you feel comfortable and happy.

Tools to help us manage our anxieties:

- Do not try to "keep it a secret." I advise you to get help and work on renewal.

- Get professional advice.

- If your medical doctor or psychiatrist prescribes medication, know all the facts. Learn the side-effects and addiction possibilities that some medications can carry.

- Remember, "the only thing we have to fear is fear itself" (Franklin D. Roosevelt).

- Be humble and admit that you do not have your "act together."

- Be accountable. Find an accountability person that you can openly discuss your anxiety with. Ask this person to coach you and support you as you learn how to handle tough anxiety yourself.

- Do not get side-tracked and work on the things that help you work through anxiety.

- Learn to maintain a journal. Write down your extreme moments of anxiety and how you worked through the experience.

- Do not worry about what you cannot control.

- Work on discovering the true you. You will learn quite a lot about yourself this way.

- Use intuition over intellect, and always trust it.

- Regain your control.

- Last but not least, let me repeat, find someone who will always keep you accountable.

Chapter Seven

When Panic Attacks

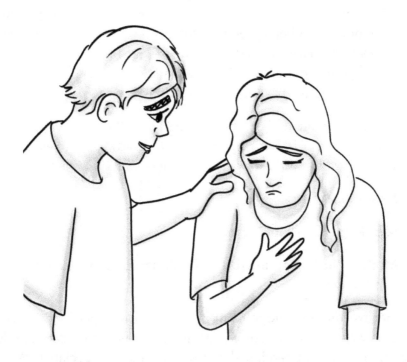

Once, my parents and I were traveling in Corpus Christi, Texas. We were meeting my older brother there, who was serving in the Navy. His ship, the USS Bushnell, was coming into the harbor for a couple of days. He had been out to sea for about a year, and I was ecstatic to see him. As a bonus, we were allowed to go on a ship tour of the USS Bushnell as well.

There was a fantastic seafood restaurant that we had visited several times before in Corpus Christi. It was one of our favorite places in the city. Once we had settled into our seats, the four of us ordered our food from the menu. I reluctantly ordered a hamburger, knowing that I would likely choke on it. You guessed it; I convinced myself that I would choke, and I choked. This time it was really severe.

Unintentionally, I made quite a scene in the restaurant with my choking episode. I was completely embarrassed, especially because of my brother's presence. My brother was unaware of my anxieties and unaccustomed to being around little kids. I had my way of "getting under his skin," one way or another. My panic attacks added to the barrier of our relationship.

I shared in an earlier chapter many of the challenges with anxiety I dealt with during my fourth-grade year. Yes, panic attacks played a significant part in my personal living hell.

I hate panic attacks!

Me: "Mama, I'm choking to death!"

Mother: "Just calm down, and don't panic. Go to the restroom and spit it out."

Her words did little to calm me down. I was petrified, scared that I was going to choke to death. This time, our family practitioner recommended that I see an allergy specialist. What did this specialist do? He ran me through a series of allergy tests. One test was a "skin test." I sat in a room, and the doctor and his nurse placed an allergen on my back. Eventually, he or a nurse pricked my skin to determine all the things that I might be allergic to. This was a blast… NOT! It was enough to drive anyone into a panic attack. So unsurprisingly, I had another panic attack.

Symptoms of a Panic Attack

• Racing or irregular heartbeat (palpitations)

• Trembling

- Shortness of breath (hyperventilation)

- A choking sensation

- Nausea

- Dizziness

- Tingling fingers

- Ringing in your ears

- Sweating

These symptoms can vary from person to person. Individuals who experience panic attacks do not necessarily experience each symptom at the same time. If you experience panic attacks, you can get better at recognizing them. You can also improve how you work with them and through them. Often, panic attacks get fewer as time moves on. You start becoming more secure and conquering fears that have been your foe.

Crawling Under the Bed or the Desk is a Symptom, Not a Cure

Crawling under my bed when intense anxiety seemed to overpower me.

When I was a young boy, crawling under my bed was my hiding place. This was a practice I followed until I was about eight years old. Several things made me fearful and induced in me what I call a pre-panic attack.

When I knew that I did something terrible and deserved a confrontation with my mother, I would run and hide under my bed.

My mother was one of the most remarkable individuals that I have ever known. She was very balanced with me, and she somewhat understood my emotional anxiety. I was never diagnosed with an anxiety disorder by medical professionals, which is not surprising in retrospect. This baffled many doctors, and it was seemingly a challenge to pinpoint what all of my issues were.

I overheard doctors telling my mother that I was a sensitive, insecure, nice kid and a slow learner. I know they did not have any ill intent, but the sheer ignorance and callousness with which they made remarks like that, without thinking of the psychological ramifications, is stunning.

What understanding did I derive from their comments about me being a "nice kid" who had "difficulty learning?" That I was delicate in mind and that I was dumb. Thankfully, my mother was able to understand that I needed love, security, and above all, patience. It was difficult for us to respect what these medical "professionals" had to say.

I would run to hide under my bed when a lady came to give my mother a hair perm.

A little bizarre, right? You are thinking, "Dude, you really had some issues!" You are right, as I did indeed have some "issues." There was something about the smell of the hair perms that made me fearful of them, though I could not pinpoint exactly what it was about them.

I also found the bed was a great hiding place for me when someone that I did not like came to visit my elder brothers.

Thankfully, this was not a great number of people, to begin with. There was something about two of these men that was personally threatening to me. These guys never did anything to harm me, but I felt that they were capable of doing it if they chose. I may have had good intuition as a boy.

Oddly, a couple of these men proved later in life to not exactly be the greatest people for our society. One of these men was a friend of my oldest brother. Years later, this man went into a drunken and drugged rage, and killed both his father and mother. This was crazy and saddening but proved to me that I should follow my gut instinct.

Crawling under my desk during adulthood.

I crawled under my desk in my office one time. I wanted to do it again many times afterward but managed to hold myself back from doing it. Who wants to admit that kind of thing, right? Well, I admit it.

This incident occurred sometime in 2003. I was the lead pastor of our church. Eight months in succession, countless terrible deaths occurred in our congregation. People that I was very close to and loved greatly died. The deaths came out of nowhere. Several of these fatalities were due to car accidents of young adults. Some deaths were by disease, whereas two deaths were by cancer, with the last one being the death of my mother. I was the officiant of each funeral service, excluding my mother's service for obvious reasons. Regardless, all of this, coupled with the daily pressures of trying to pastor people, an unforgettable mark was left on my mental state.

I had ministered to hundreds of people that experienced tragedy in their families. What was different this time around? My mother's death was expected, so we still had time to prepare ourselves for it. Three years earlier, she was diagnosed with multiple myeloma. The pressure and stress of events in my personal life and church ministry played a crucial role in my anxiety.

In those months of tragedy, when the church's office phone rang, I wanted to run away. I would hear the phone ring and actually stop whatever I was doing. Sometimes, I would secretly trot out of the office to escape outside. Other times, I would leave the office and get into my vehicle and drive around for a while. Other times I would contemplate hiding under my desk. One day

73

the office phone rang, and I got down on the floor and crawled under the desk. I stayed there until I felt like the coast was clear - until the phone stopped ringing. It is very agonizing to have to re-think these events for this book – but re-think them, I must.

It did not take a rocket scientist to know that I needed some professional help. Given the position of leadership I was in, who do you go to for help that is also discreet? Other than my wife, I did not even have a friend that I could trust completely and undoubtedly. Most of my friendships were in the church, of which I was the pastor — a bit of a conflict of interest. I was their spiritual leader, not their best friend. I had been a pastor in this church for many years by that time.

Over time, people had overlooked some of the wrong decisions I had made. There were indeed some wonderful people in the congregation, but there were also judgmental influences among some about my family. I did not believe that I had anyone in the assembly of couple-thousand attendees that I could altogether trust with zero reservations.

Some things that I did to correct my situation:

I continued all my duties, including Sunday speaking obligations and leading our staff. The congregation was thoroughly well-cared for by the pastoral and administrative staff. I found it necessary to stand back for a while, to regroup and emotionally heal from some activities.

I stopped working with families that had lost loved ones.

I stopped officiating funerals for some time.

I stopped making hospital visits.

I did very little family or pastoral marital counseling.

I began seeking professional guidance and counseling for myself.

After some while, these things provided some much-needed relief. My anxiety disorder stayed complicated for several years. This chapter in my life eventually became tornadic. Time does not allow me to explain. Rearranging my schedule did help. It did not completely heal, nor did it bring strength in a really bad environment, either.

Panic Attacks can still Happen to Me

If you have not had panic attacks, the chance of you having one now is slim. I am not immune to having a panic attack myself. Not too long ago, my wife and I were traveling by car during an extremely heavy rainstorm. It was as though the rain was falling down in uninterrupted sheets of water. Traffic was heavy, and there were no highway exits for miles in either direction. There was no place to turn, and it was unsafe to pull off onto the shoulder of the highway, too. Strangely, I felt a panic attack rising to the surface.

Once a person has had a panic attack, they are easy to recognize the next time around. You can prepare yourself before they hit. I began to rehearse mentally, *Take control, there's no place to go.* Once again, *Take control, there's no place to go.* Again, *Take control, there's no place to go.* After repeating it to myself several times, the panic feelings dissipated on their own.

Some Encouragement
Should You Have Reoccurring Panic Attacks

Remember that panic attacks are usually short in duration. Normally, anywhere from a few minutes to twenty minutes. Also, rest assured that your body knows how to handle a panic attack and how to reboot in their aftermath. Dr. Alice Boyes, Ph.D., says, "There is no one in the history of the planet whose anxiety system has ever become stuck in panic attack mode permanently. It's a physiological impossibility." Her book, *The Anxiety Toolkit*, is a fantastic read.

Generally, a panic attack will stop by itself. A panic attack is not a mental breakdown. The panic attack victim feels as if "Big Foot" or the "Loch Ness Monster" is stalking them. The fear seems overwhelming, but it is definitely possible to overcome them. So remember that you can be the overcomer.

> **PLEASE UNDERSTAND THAT YOU ARE NOT YOUR PANIC ATTACK. A PANIC ATTACK IS AN *EVENT*; IT IS NOT A *LIFESTYLE*.**

If you have a panic attack, there are a number of tactics you can deploy. A few of the most important ones are listed below. These are not intended to be in any certain order:

1. Breath slow, as you might have a tendency to hyperventilate.

2. Talk to yourself; tell yourself that you will be okay.

3. Try to change the setting or change the temperature by moving somewhere else.

4. Some people have success by stroking their arms with their hands.

5. Get a medical check-up as soon as possible if you have not seen a doctor about your anxiety disorder before. If you have a medical disorder, it is entirely possible that the techniques I have listed may not help you. Preventative healthcare is the best form of healthcare, after all.

6. Take control of your diet. Limit the intake of sweeteners, alcohol, caffeine, or tobacco. These things could become seriously problematic to your condition in the long-term.

No one controls the market of understanding, nor all the tools to become anxiety free. There is no monopoly of ideas to overcome anxiety. Experiment to find out the best ways to manage your anxiety until you eventually discover what suits you best.

To close out this chapter on panic attacks, I want to share with you a great technique that I have come across. Barry McDonagh is the author of the book *DARE*. In it, he explains, "The DARE Response," which is an approach that is the result of his own personal healing of anxiety.

The DARE Response

Scaling away the fear from sensations that you feel is the secret to ending panic attacks altogether.

First, when you feel the anxiety of a panic attack approaching, respond with "so what?" or "whatever."

Second, as soon as the strength of the anxiety is felt and identified, "accept and allow" the uncomfortable feelings, as well as the disturbing thoughts.

Third, if the anxiety peaks into a panic attack, "run toward it." Conversely, do not run from it.

Fourth, when the flood of adrenaline successfully passes, there may be a few more similar floods to follow. Allow your body to experience the normal sensations of the attack then…

Fifth, engage fully with the anxiety. Tell yourself, "I'm excited by this feeling. Bring it on!"

The Four Steps of DARE are:

Defuse – Instead of saying, "What if," say, "So what?"

Allow it – By accepting the anxious feeling, move with it.

Run toward – By telling yourself that you feel excited by your anxious feelings.

Engage – Focus on something that engages your mind, like a book or a task.

These suggestions, tools, and techniques can help you "win" in your battle with panic attacks. Do not be ashamed of your anxiety, nor your panic attacks. You are going to learn how to defeat them and move forward with more peace and freedom in your life.

As you refresh your personal approach to anxiety, others will cross your path, people who are fellow-strugglers. You will be empowered to reach out to them and add value to their life. You will feel rewarded, as your story has helped someone move toward success over anxiety.

Chapter Eight

The Monster of Bitterness

I allowed many years of going through stress, anxiety, and panic attacks to make me vulnerable to being hurt. I have spent the majority of my adult life trying to help people heal from emotional wounds. All this led me to discover a critical cycle in emotional anxiety. It goes somewhat as follows:

Relational *hurt* can lead to *the development of anger.*

Anger can lead to the appearance of *resentment.*

If there is no resolve or forgiveness, *bitterness will follow* suit. Bitterness is a viciously malignant poison, and it will shape our thoughts and our perspective on life and people. The danger of bitterness is found in a pity party that you and I create, after which we eventually invite others to join our party.

At our pity party, we consciously or subconsciously attempt to spread the virus or disease of bitterness to others. Usually, we are completely unaware of the toxic poison we are spreading.

Rick Warren, the lead pastor of Saddleback Church in Lake Forest, California, has said on numerous occasions, "Hurt people – hurt people." I have seen this statement come true far too many times for me to have any doubt about it. It has been true in my life, as well as many others that I have known.

It is quite normal for a person suffering from anxiety and depression to want others to feel their pain. I wanted someone to understand my hurt. Whenever I would meet with someone who I thought might step along-side me and help me in some way, I would want them to understand my pain. As we would talk, I felt something inside of me, almost crying out, "Help me, Help me, Help me." I realize that this sounds selfish. Every person wants someone to identify with them. Unfortunately, I never found the words nor the transparency to share my burden or express my feelings to most of those people. I was hurt, and I wanted help from a good samaritan.

Someone has said, "There are always two sides to every story." This means there is your side of the story, and then there is my side of the story. Well, personally, I think there are three sides to every story. There is your side of the story, and there is my side of the story, and then there is the truth somewhere out there. Your side of the story and my side of the story are actually our perceptions of what took place. Perceptions are mostly slanted. What actually happened is always something different altogether.

My side of the story…

I went through the cycle of emotions that was mentioned above:

Hurt

Anger

Resentment

Bitterness

Of course, this is according to my perspective. Since that chapter in my life, I have been able to sort through some life-changing things. This has given me not only emotional freedom, but I have also been able to forgive some people. These individuals had no idea that I was bitter with them. Now, the issues are not important for me to list in this writing. In fact, so much of it was the state of mind that I found myself in.

I will name my state of mind, "Numbness." Due to the hurt, anger, and resentment, my mind was hemorrhaging a barrage of emotions. These emotions eventually developed into bitterness. I found myself lying in bitterness, and it was so deep and so thick that I refused to admit my condition. This is how I eventually found this monster of bitterness that had overwhelmed my life.

The Uninvited Guest Named Anger

Rarely do most people associate the emotion of anger with that of anxiety. Frequently, the anxious person is a caring and loving person. This person is an over-achiever that tries to help others. How does someone like this allow anger to creep into the dwelling of their mind's crevices?

Some believe anger is the primary emotion of anxiety. It appears that when anger overcomes any one of us, there will be serious health consequences. On this connection, the American Psychological Association has published:

"These 'terrible twos' increase vulnerability to illnesses, especially upper respiratory illness; compromise the immune system, increase lipid levels, exacerbate pain, and increase the risk of death from cardiovascular disease and from all sources of death."

I know that when I get angry, I try to internalize it. I simply do not like confrontation, which is why I hold it inside myself. This is a personal fault. I was taught as a child: "Don't show your anger. When you look angry, you look ugly." People do not want to experience the consequence of our anger. Mostly, we have been taught to suppress our feelings of anger. Anger can become like a time-bomb. Its explosion can occur at any given moment. However, anger does not have to be an ugly emotion at all. Nevertheless, it still needs to be discussed and dealt with properly.

Continued suppression of anger will lead some people to a place of shame and embarrassment. At the school, the ball field, the church, and the workplace, all sorts of things will happen that can tempt anyone to explode in a fit of anger. If we cannot work out the anger, we will complicate things. We allow anger to eat us internally. Open displays of anger are unacceptable in most public places.

Someone might see our display of anger as a threat.

We frighten people.

It is socially unaccepted.

People may not appreciate our transparency.

Others may avoid us after a confrontation.

Of course, I am aware that there are other repercussions for being open and discussing our anger in public. Our society has been labeled by some as the "Laodicean Culture." What this means is that people are encouraged to speak out for their rights, and yet it seems unaccepted for someone to express anger.

There is no One Size Fits All to Expressions of Anger

We all express our anger in different ways, but we ought to always be respectful to the person we are angry with. More importantly than that, we should try our best to be clear-headed and make sure we are not angry at the wrong person. I was an overhead crane operator in my early twenties. The cranes that I operated were about 30-40 feet above the floor of a large steel manufacturing plant. Every weekday, we lifted several tons of steel into the air while people below us would grind the edges and weld units together.

As an overhead crane operator, I would follow the directions of someone far below on the floor, guiding me through hand signals. They would signal how I ought to move a large tank or a 10-ton piece of metal for welding. It would take me 1 or 2 seconds to stop a crane's operations once they had been set in motion. Sometimes, a man would get angry and look up at me while I was in the crane and begin yelling. Some would use profanity and call me names that I obviously did not appreciate.

Once, on a day that had been going smoothly, a man directed me to move an object in the other direction abruptly. The crane was already in motion. Unfortunately, due to technical reasons, I did not stop the crane's movement fast enough.

He began screaming at me ridiculously. This guy was using expletives that I would not put in print.

When I was able to park the crane and climb down, I approached this man and told him, "Hey, when you have something to say to me, treat me respectfully. I am not a machine. When you motion for me to stop the crane, it takes one to two seconds for the momentum to stop." From that moment on, I never had an issue with that man.

Ways to Manage Anger

1. Realize that you are angry.

2. Accept that anger is not wrong or bad, but rather it is a natural reaction.

3. Learn how to express your anger without being belligerent or defensive.

4. Think before you speak or act.

5. Come to terms with the hurt and wounds that others have inflicted upon you. This starts with childhood wounds and hurts. Then, it addresses the hurts and wounds that were inflicted upon us during our teen years into adulthood.

6. Receive therapy or counseling to learn to manage your anger better.

7. Practice treating others respectfully. This will teach your offender how to treat you better, as well.

8. Learn your "rights!" There is the right place, the right time, the right way, and the right person.

Bitterness Wants Someone Else to Hurt

When you and I taste something that is bitter, we usually make a face and occasionally spit it out. Have you ever tasted something that tastes bad, and then you look at someone near you and say, "Hey, I dare you to taste this!" Why do we want them to taste it? Because we want someone to suffer the same bad taste that we went through. We are strange creatures, are we not? When we feel offended or violated in some way, we inherently want someone that caused the pain to suffer, too.

Symptoms of Resentment and Bitterness and How to Fix Them

Resentment and bitterness can sweep across our hearts and our minds, taking over our thought process. It takes root inside of us before we know what has overtaken us. There is not necessarily any distinct order to the symptoms of bitterness. Here are some things to notice in this respect:

- *Jealousy* – Someone got a reward, a raise, a compliment, or perhaps a promotion at work, but you did not. Those feelings of "I am not happy for them" saturate your mind. Eventually, your jealousy will show.

  ○Fix it – Find the motivation to achieve whatever it is that you are looking to accomplish in life. Set up your own goals, and do not expect anything to be handed over to you. Work hard towards achieving it.

- Negativity – Bitterness causes us to see the wrongs until it spreads to the seat of our emotions. We become cynical, and people simply do not enjoy being around us when we are like that.

  ○Fix it – Look in the mirror and tell yourself to stop being critical. Do not be your own worst enemy. Look at the good things in life, and when you feel like you have been cheated, count your blessings. No matter how bad it is for you, remind yourself that it could be much worse. It is all up to you.

- Resentment – Resentment is the step right before bitterness. Realize and admit when you resent someone. It is

85

messing up your mind. You cannot simultaneously hold resentment and have a healthy mindset about life and the future.

  ° Fix it - Forgive them, you may be unable to forget, but forgiveness will release you from the inner turmoil and pain. You are not released until you release your offender. Do not do it for their sake. Rather, do it for your sake and for the sake of those around you.

• Bitterness – It started as a hurt until it worked into anger. Eventually, it moved into resentment, and now it is rooted in your mind. Bitterness loves to bathe itself in perceived injustice.

Psychology Today contributor and blogger Stephen Diamond, Ph.D., says that bitterness is a "chronic and pervasive state of smoldering resentment." I agree wholeheartedly with that statement. The bitterness I held towards some individuals in the past carried forward in my heart. For ten years, I was held captive by these feelings. How can I know if I am bitter with someone? Let me tell you the way I found out, and you can, too.

How to know if I am bitter at someone:

See the person in public, consider what you feel when you see them.

Let this person's name be mentioned. What are your thoughts about them?

Pray for this person, as well as what you feel. Your first prayer may be, "God, give Bill a sucky day." That is alright; keep praying for them, and your prayers may completely change.

The Price of Bitterness

Bitterness has a massive price to pay. Part of the price of bitterness includes but is not limited to:

Prolonged mental pain.

Depression.

Insomnia.

Distrust.

Wounded relationships.

Health problems, such as high blood pressure, back pain, headaches, etc.

Feeling victimized instead of moving past the offense and pain.

Bitterness, which hurts those around you because it creeps into current relationships.

Blindness to your shortcomings.

WE FIND EMOTIONAL HEALING WITH RESENTMENT BY FORGIVING.

This is how we find healing with bitterness:

1. Talk about the hurt, pain, anger, and resentment.

2. Admit to the bitterness.

3. Decide that you are not "emotionally free," and that the act of someone else enslaves you.

4. Admit that the person that offended you may not deserve to be forgiven.

5. Realize that you are not "getting back" at the offender. They are going free.

6. Resolve that you want freedom from that person and their wounds.

7. Realize that you have also hurt people and that you are not perfect.

How to release the offender:

Pray for this person.

Write a letter with all of your pain and offenses (but do not send the letter).

Forgive and release this person(s). You do not have to be friends with this person again. Indeed, it may be extremely unwise to do so.

If bitter feelings remain, rehearse this exercise. Do this over and over until you feel at peace.

Chapter Nine

The God Factor

Now, I have no idea what your spiritual beliefs are. Perhaps you do not consider yourself a Christian. In fact, perhaps you do not believe in any organized religion at all. Please know that no matter what it is that you believe, I fully respect and support your right to your personal beliefs. I would never attempt to shame you for them, nor would I think less of you if you do not believe in God or if your faith is different from mine.

If you wish to continue to read this segment of the book, I sincerely hope that you will do so with an open attitude, too. Most of what I write comes from my personal experience; it is framed by who I am as a person. Being a heartfelt Christian, my faith has influenced me a lot. Hence, it is my hope that you will be able to glean the heart behind the writing.

Feeling Less Than a Christian? You Are Not Alone

Soon after I resigned from my position as the lead pastor of the church, a place I had ministered to for over 25 years, I attended a local function. There, I saw another pastor who also served for many years in the same town, albeit at another local church. We eventually bumped into each other and began talking, and during the conversation, I shared some of the guilt I carried.

I explained how I felt guilty about taking medications for anxiety and depression. This pastor-friend looked at me right in the eyes and said, "Don, I could tell you of six other pastors in our city that are also taking medication for an anxiety disorder." The concern in his voice was intense. I stood there for a few moments looking at him, and then I said, "I had no idea that there were others." He smiled encouragingly and replied, "Don, you are not alone."

It is easy for many to harbor guilt over their anxiety, especially when the person in question comes from a church background. Unfortunately, the guilt can intensify when one takes medications for this disorder, and it can multiply exponentially for a Christian leader. This leader is tempted to feel "all alone," believing that no one is capable of understanding them.

If you ever feel alone or feel as though you are the "only one" around who is suffering from anxiety, then please understand that what you are believing is an utter lie. We are not supposed to face anxiety alone. Do not allow yourself to become isolated like this. It is extremely unhealthy to try to do life all alone and not reaching out for help when you need it. I had people all around me. My wife and my children were always ready to help me if I asked. I served with a great staff, along with some fantastic people in the church. Many years ago, I heard Zig Ziggler say, "It's lonely at the top." Now I know that is true.

The leader of any organization will be called upon to make leadership decisions. The leader will carry the bulk of the responsibility, and that is the part that can leave one feeling lonely. Being lonely at the top should not mean that we live in isolation from people. Living a life quarantined from everyone, and everything is certainly not recommended. Conversely, staying true to one's self for a prolonged period is an unhealthy practice for anyone.

Spiritual Questions that People Have about Anxiety

No one is immune to anxiety disorders. This includes those who consider themselves dedicated, practicing Christians. Many anxiety sufferers have sincere questions they wish they could ask God. These are questions such as:

God, are you angry at me?

No, God is not angry with you. God loves you unconditionally.

Should I deny my anxiety since I am a Christian?

No, do not deny your anxiety. Rather, accept it, embrace it, and learn to control it.

Do I have this mental health issue because I am being punished?

No, God is not punishing you. In fact, He wants you to acknowledge that He is with you amid all your anxieties.

Do I have this emotional disorder because I am a terrible person?

No, you are not a terrible person if you have anxieties. I have already stated that you are separate from your anxiety. You are not your anxiety. Do not let it define you.

Will I ever conquer anxiety, or is it going to be there forever?

Yes, you can barricade anxiety from controlling you. No, you may not overcome anxiety altogether. I have provided management techniques that you can practice during these testing times of anxiety.

Anxiety Can Lead a Person to do Stupid Things

One day, I had anxiety hammering on all four walls of my mind. It was more than I could contain. A man on our pastoral staff made a comment that moved my emotions to unqualified anger. I abruptly stood up, and with my right arm, I tried to plunge my fist through the table that we were all sitting around. The noise was loud, and my actions led all seven or eight pastors' jaws to drop and look on amazed. I purposely hid the agonizing pain throbbing from my hand, all the way up my arm and into my chest. I immediately knew that I had broken something, and it was not the table that I had hit.

Despite the searing pain, I kept my composure and slowly sat down and continued with the meeting. I kept my hand under the table on my lap. I did not want anyone to see me look at my hand, so I did not even glance at it. I had too much pride to admit that I was in agony. At the moment, I did not have a desire to acknowledge my childishness, let alone apologize for it.

I allowed some thirty minutes to pass, and then I excused myself to go to the restroom. As soon as I closed the door behind me, I grabbed my right-hand with my left-hand. The hand that I tried to use as a club was in unbearable, throbbing pain. I did everything except cry. I examined the damage to my hand. My right hand was about twice the size it normally was, and the color was a grotesque mixture of black, blue, and bright red. I carefully placed the hand under cold running water. After I had gained my composure and washed my face, I rushed back to the meeting.

92

I took a moment and admitted that I foolishly lost my temper in frustration. Then, I apologized to everyone for my outburst. Yes, it was "show and tell" time. I laid my hand out on the table for everyone to see the results of my childish display. One of our pastors said, "I knew that your hand must be hurting beyond belief. Either you are holding back the pain, or you are a tough old dude."

I replied, "Actually, it's both, I am in pain, and I am just one tough old dude. So, don't try me." Everyone laughed at the situation. I do not make any excuses for my behavior that day.

I want to share some of the things I was battling that seemed to have gone out of control. My pastoral responsibilities included:

*Leading staff in weekly planning.

*Leading the staff and church by vision casting.

*Sermon series preparation.

*Sermon writing.

*Preaching and teaching.

*Counseling and ministering to people.

*Community missions coordination.

*Planning and leading foreign mission trips.

There is more to the background of this chaotic scenario. I was responsible for raising money and funding the building of a 20,000 square feet auditorium. It took five years to accomplish this, from the day of the promoting and planning phase, until the day that it was completed and open for use.

The building contractor estimated the total cost of the new structure to be at about 1.85 million dollars. The church secured a loan for this amount. This company's architects drew the plans, but the price was over-budgeted for the things that we wanted. We left this company. Later, we went into mediation with them to pay for damages.

The church hired a new construction company. This company guaranteed they could build the building we wanted. The project was scheduled to meet our 1.85-million-dollar budget. We had to dismiss this contractor for overspending on the budget and obtained a bank loan for more funding to complete the project.

Soon after we released that company, we hired a new building supervisor. He was a good man and very capable of leading us to complete the building. However, he was unable to lead us to completion within the current stressed budget.

This gentleman had to be replaced. Finally, the fourth construction manager led the church to a finished building. The completed project had a final price of around 3.3 million dollars. We were extremely over budget on the building, to say the least.

Our congregation consisted of a couple of thousand people. There was also a quandary of turmoil happening behind the scenes. People are people, and sometimes there will be issues such as gossip and affairs. This church was no different.

I was experiencing some serious health issues at the time. Resolving them included a couple of surgeries. To add to the mixture of misfortune, we also had some family issues, of which I will not go into detail. All families have their struggles as the kids get older and make unwise decisions. Pastors' families are no different.

My wife and I continued our personal relationship with God daily. I attempted to be the best husband and best dad that I knew how to be. My mother lived in our home during this time, until one day, when she suddenly passed away. I would not have missed this opportunity to have my mother in our home for anything.

God is good all the time. He is loving, and He is faithful. Even with faith, and maintaining a relationship with God, 'stuff happens.' The stuff that happened added pressure, stress, and anxiety to my wife, our children, and of course to me. Everything became almost more than I could handle.

Several Bible verses gave me strength. When all the pressure, stress, and anxiety overwhelmed me, God's word gave me the ability to cope. There have been countless times when I have not been the model Christian or exemplary pastor, yet my God has never left me, nor has he ever failed me.

God is not Silent on the Subject of Anxiety

One of the most quoted Bible passages is located in the book of Philippians, in chapter 4, verses 6 and 7. This is what it says, "Do not be anxious about anything, but in every situation, by prayer and petition, with thanksgiving, present your requests to God. 7 And the peace of God, which transcends all understanding, will guard your hearts and your minds in Christ Jesus" (NIV).

Key action items from this passage are:

- Do not be anxious about anything.

- In every situation, pray and petition or tell God what you need.

- Thank Him as you make your requests.

God's promises in this passage are:

- You will experience God's peace.

- God's peace will surpass your understanding.

• This peace will guard your heart and mind.

Also, in the New Testament, specifically in the book of I Peter, chapter 5, verse 7, we read, "Cast all your anxiety on him because he cares for you" (NIV).

The take away from this verse is:

Cast or throw all your anxiety onto God.

God cares for you.

Anxiety Increases When We Carry Things We Aren't Supposed to Carry

You may be crying out something like, "This anxiety is more than I can carry, and it is destroying my life and my family."

> **YOU MAY BE WONDERING WHERE GOD IS IN ALL OF YOUR CHAOS.**

Or you may not even be sure if you believe that God is real or if he truly cares for you. Jesus Christ proves to us that he really does care. He came willingly and sacrificed his life on the cross for each of us. The cross of Jesus was proof that He was more than willing to carry each one of us.

Jesus said, "Come to me, all you who are weary and burdened, and I will give you rest." (Matthew 11:28)

He made it clear:

Come to Him all who are weary (tired, stressed, anxious, fearful)

He will give you rest (rest of the mind, body, and soul).

Sometimes, you and I carry our anxieties because we simply refuse to trust God to help us. Will you allow Jesus to carry you when you cannot carry yourself?

1. Trust Him and give Him your anxiety, your stress, and your weariness.

2. You are not alone, so stop trying to do life alone.

3. See a counselor.

4. Find a good local church of people who are not your judge, and they admit to being your fellow strugglers.

What is a Christian?

First, let us define the word Christian. The word "Christian" is a word that was given to followers of Jesus Christ. The term was a distinct term from Judaism. The Bible says, "The disciples were called Christians, first in Antioch" (Recorded in Acts 11:26). This group of Christ-followers was Christ-like in their daily ways of life.

How can Someone Become a Christian?

Christians believe that Jesus is the Son of God and that He was crucified. He was crucified, not for His sins and wrong, but rather for the sins and transgressions of mankind. Christians believe that Christ rose from death three days after His burial. Anyone that places their trust in Christ will have His eternal salvation. Believe in His sacrificial act of redemption on the cross and tell Him that you want Him in your life.

"FOR WHOSOVER WILL CALL UPON THE NAME OF THE LORD, SHALL BE SAVED" (ROMANS 10:13).

Observe these four steps to receiving Christ into your life:

1. *Admit* that you have sinned or wronged God.

2. *Believe* that Jesus Christ took your place and died on the cross. He paid for all the bad things that you and I have done.

3. *Confess* to Jesus that you believe and that you want Him to come into your life.

4. *Ask* Him to come into your life.

"Dear God, I believe that Jesus died on the cross for me and that He rose again. I know that I have wronged you and that you are a forgiving God. I ask your forgiveness and I trust you to come into my life to stay. In Jesus name, amen."

"Very truly I tell you, whoever hears my word and believes Him who sent me has eternal life and will not be judged but has crossed over from death to life" (John 5:24).

Chapter Ten

The Great Depression

I was a fourth-grade boy suffering from an anxiety disorder and panic attacks. I was enduring a certain degree of depression, which was undiagnosed. As I have stated before, these were my living hell days as a young child. My mother took me to a couple of medical doctors for treatment, but neither of them knew what to do for me or do with me. My school officials just labeled me as a child with "learning disorders" or that I was just a "slow learner."

As I previously mentioned in chapter two, it was not until 1968 that any medical doctor mentioned in print any symptom similar to my disorder. *"Hyperkinetic Impulse Disorder"* first appeared in the Diagnostic Statistical Manual (DSM). Before it, nothing akin to it existed. In 1980, this disorder was renamed Attention Deficit Disorder (ADD).

Thinking about those days still brings strong emotions out of me. When I write about what I experienced or when I share these stories about my early childhood anxiety, I cringe extremely hard. I was undoubtedly a depressed little boy who was deeply misunderstood.

Since then, depression did not meet up with me again until I was an adult. At the age of 27, my wife and my four-year-old son went to a city and a church that we had served in three years prior. The first time we served in this church was as the student and worship pastor. This time, I became the lead pastor. I had conducted a lengthy enough investigation on the church to know two major things about it.

First, they were greatly in debt. Second, they did not have the greatest financial reputation in the community. Since we had served on staff in the past, we loved the people and the community. As such, we felt strongly that this was our calling. There were about 40 people who regularly attended the church. In addition to them, nearly 40 children were brought to church on buses by some extremely faithful people who served on our bus ministry. The church was over its head. They were severely in financial and attendance decline.

That Sunday, I preached twice because of "the call." The congregation voted with a 98 percent yes. Evidently, the people wanted me to become their new pastor, and our contributions totaled $525 that day.

Early the following Monday morning, one of the men from the church and I ran some essential errands. First, we went to the bank and then to the post office to retrieve the church's mail. This gentleman was a personal friend, the church treasurer, and also the deacon of the church. Neither of us had any idea of the shocking morning that was about to unfold.

There were going to be three major *stress-out events* that we were going to encounter in a period of fewer than two hours. These events stirred up some extremely *anxious moments*. Over a period of time, this affected my depression adversely. Please understand that anxiety does not necessarily lead to depression. However, it can lead to depression, as it did in my life.

Stress-Out Event #1:

We arrived at the bank to withdraw funds from the church account. After closing the account, our intention was to start things afresh at another bank. As we requested the remaining funds in the church account, I will never forget what happened next. The bank teller quickly gathered our account information and promptly informed us,

"Here are your closing funds, two cents."

She placed two pennies on the counter in front of us. Both of us exchanged a quick, embarrassed glace with the lady. My friend picked up the coins, and then we asked to speak with a bank official. Due to my previous investigation, I was aware that the bank was holding a note that was several years old. This loan was well past its due. Eventually, one of the bank officials came out and introduced himself as Mr. Bryant.

Here is the way the conversation went:

Me: "Mr. Bryant, I am Don Womble, and this is _____. I am the new pastor of _____, and I understand that the church has an outstanding loan with your bank."

Mr. Bryant: "It's a pleasure to meet you. Please, both of you have a seat. Yes, your church does have an outstanding loan with us, and I just happen to have the note in my desk."

We sat down with the bank's vice-president. He opened a bottom drawer on the right side of his desk and slowly pulled out an envelope, which had the name of the church scribbled in crude handwriting on the front. He opened the envelope and removed a slip of paper that read, "Three Thousand Five Hundred Dollars owed."

Me: "Mr. Bryant, first let me say that our congregants and we are extremely sorry that the loan is past due. I wish to work out a monthly payment agreement that is satisfactory with your bank."

Mr. Bryant: "We are also very interested in working out a payment plan. How much payment do you believe the church can comfortably afford to pay monthly?"

Me: "The total offering this weekend was $525 dollars. Since I am new here in my position, I do not know what the average weekly offerings will actually be. Nonetheless, we will agree to send at least a payment of $100 monthly."

Mr. Bryant: "Mr. Womble, if your church will send $100 monthly, we will be glad to set up that payment schedule with you. I will keep this note in my desk and ledger each payment that you send. Also, if you make the promise of this payment good, we will 'kill' the interest. When you bring the payment in or mail it to us, just place 'To the attention of Mr. Bryant,' on each payment."

Me: "We certainly thank you for working with us, and I will see to it myself that the monthly payment is sent to you on time. I have just one more thing to share (I was really nervous about this since the banker had already been so gracious with us). Mr. Bryant, we have closed our checking account with your bank. We will be opening a new church checking account at another bank."

Mr. Bryant: "I think that is an excellent idea. Let me show you something."

He opened up a file of our church that had a list of all of the returned checks, marked insufficient funds. The list of returned checks covered the past eight months of that year. There were over 80 insufficient checks in that file. The banker continued:

Mr. Bryant: "Mr. Womble, I am sad to say that your church has the worst account record at our bank. I think that you are making a wise decision to change banks."

We shook hands and left the bank. The same day, we located another bank in our city that was only six months old. We opened a new church account using the funds from Sunday's offering. If I remember correctly, I think that we also added the two cents from the previous bank account. Believe me, the anxiety was building, but there were two more major stress events to *top off* the morning.

Stress-Out Event #2:

We left our new bank and drove to the post office to pick up the church mail from the mailbox. The treasurer had the key, and as he opened the box, we were amazed. The post office box was completely stuffed with mail, like a turkey stuffed with dressing. Working together as a team, we pulled out an envelope after envelope. We approached a table in the post office lobby to sort out the mail and began sifting through the "bills or statements" from advertisements. We began to add up all the account payables, and they totaled somewhere around $11,000. Now, just imagine how we were feeling at that moment. The church had $525.02 to "its name," and we were already over $10,475 in the "red." We were two overwhelmed, young men.

We went to our car and drove away from the post office in dismay. We did not have much to say on our way as we drove to my friend's house. We arrived at his home and slowly walked in.

No sooner had we sat down in his living room when his wife told us that the church secretary needs me to contact her ASAP.

Stress-Out Event #3:

Here we were on a Monday, close to 10:30 A.M. I called the secretary. This was before the release of cell phones to the public. The secretary informed me that a man called the church office from a church bond company in Dallas, Texas. The gentleman stated that he needed to speak to the new pastor immediately.

Back up in time...

I want to back up to about two weeks prior to our arrival to speak at this church. I had located a bond company and called them. They confirmed that they were the custodian to the bondholders and that they had invested financially in building churches and owning them. Due to privacy laws, they only shared enough for me to know that the church had indebtedness.

Back to the story...

I called the man from the bond company. When he answered the phone, this is how the conversation went.

Me: "Mr. Smith, this is Don Womble, and I am the new pastor of _____. Our secretary said that you had called and need to speak to me."

Mr. Smith: "Mr. Womble, congratulations on your new position at _____. I have some very important information to share with you. Please grab a pen and paper because I need you to take notes."

Me: "Yes, sir, I am ready to hear what you have to say."

Mr. Smith: "I hope that you are sitting down, for what I am going to tell you may be a little unsettling for you as the new pastor of this church."

Me: "I am seated. Please continue."

Mr. Smith: "Pastor, did you know that your church is up for sale? The "Deed of Trust" has been placed on the bulletin board of the county courthouse in Cleburne, Texas. Pastor, your church is behind on three monthly bond installments, and it will be auctioned off to the highest bidder on the second Tuesday of this coming October."

I am glad that I was sitting down because with all the stress and anxiety of the morning, I could have curled into a fetal position when I heard that news.

Me: "Mr. Smith, your company can't do this. I have just become the pastor of the church. Please give me a chance to make things right."

Mr. Smith: "Does your church have $9,000?"

Me: "No, sir, we have $525.02!"

Mr. Smith: "Well, pastor, we not only can do this, but we are doing this."

Me: "Six weeks is not enough time. I haven't even resigned from my current position of the church where I am serving in Midland, Texas. We will not be moved to the metroplex for another two weeks. What can I do to stop this?"

Mr. Smith: "Mr. Womble, I don't believe that there is anything that you can do to stop this short of a miracle."

Me: "What if we send you money every week for the next six weeks? We will send you between $400 - $600 every week for the next six weeks. If we do this, will you remove our 'deed of trust' from the county bulletin board for auction?"

Mr. Smith: "Pastor, I can't guarantee it. However, if you send that amount of money for the next six weeks, we might be able to do something."

Me: "We will send the money and place it to your attention."

Well, as they say in the game of baseball, "Strike 1, strike 2, strike 3, you are OUT!" I was certainly out of it mentally for the moment. The *three stress-out events* occurred by 11:00 am, which was my first Monday on the job. Yet, I actually was not on the job.

Now, the next big thing was for me to attempt to explain all of this to my wife. Can you imagine being a 27-year-old man, excited about his first lead-pastor position? I had served around six years in a vocational ministry as an assistant pastor.

My faithful wife loved me and followed me basically to the end of our little world up to that point. Yes, she even followed me to the edge of the cliff that day. We left to go home that afternoon and drove 300 miles back to Midland, Texas. The next step was to resign ourselves from what had been a very comfortable lifestyle. About twelve days later, we packed up and moved towards the fearful unknown, near Fort Worth, Texas.

Did I go into depression? Not at that point. Frankly, I was fearful to some extent, but I was nonetheless bold and vibrant in my faith. I knew that God loved the people in that disarrayed church. Moreover, many people in the city needed God and a changed life. I did not understand how, but I believed in all my young heart that God would take care of it.

The conclusion to these events...

God did take care of it. After two years of being the lead pastor of the church, an agreement was signed. We developed a church bond program with the current bondholders under which there was a 10-year promise to pay everyone the money owed. Moreover, there was an added feature to this. Besides the principal owed, we paid the bondholders an additional 10-12 percent in interest. The congregation accepted the challenge of a capital funding program.

During those ten years, we paid our debtors back in monthly payments. Eight years into our agreement, the church paid all bondholders in full. Yes, God did take care of it as we took care of our financial and spiritual responsibilities.

Anxiety and Depression Are Not the Same

Some who experience depression are capable of having similar symptoms as those who have anxiety disorders. Each condition has its own emotional and behavioral symptoms.

IT IS IMPORTANT TO UNDERSTAND THAT ANXIETY IS THE SUPREME PREDICTOR OF DEPRESSION.

Nearly one-half of those diagnosed with depression also experience an anxiety disorder. Often times, anxiety sufferers with depression will have a history of anxiety disorders. Depression is a disorder of the brain, and various factors are encouraging this, such as:

Psychological factors

Environmental factors

Biological factors

Genetic factors

Depression can happen at any age. Most often, it can begin when a person grows into their teen or young adult years. As a side note, depression is more common in women.

Some Facts About Depression

The Anxiety and Depression Association of America (ADAA) says that 322 million people worldwide live with depression. According to the National Institute of Mental Health (NIMH), there are various forms of depression that affect 19 million teens and adults in the United States. They are slightly different as they can develop with unique circumstances, for example:

- *Persistent depressive disorder* (also called dysthymia). This depression will exist for up to two years. Symptoms can range from severe to less severe depression.

- *Seasonal affective disorder*. This form of depression usually begins when there is less natural sunlight available. This is typical during the winter months. Symptoms include things like sleeping more, withdrawal from social activities, and weight gain. The winter months change the disorder, even though a person can return to depression the following winter season.

- *Postpartum depression*. This depression can be confused with normal depression symptoms. Postpartum depression is a significant form of depression and usually occurs during pregnancy or after delivery.

- *Psychotic depression*. This is another severe type of depression. It is a form of psychosis, which can include delusions or hallucinations. The symptoms for psychotic depression are commonly grouped by themes, such as guilt, sickness, or poverty.

- *Bipolar disorders.* Oddly, this is different from depression. Yet, it is still frequently grouped with depression. Those with this disorder have low mood swings that eventually become major, affecting a person's life. This major depression is referred to as "bipolar depression." Persons with bipolar disorders experience "extreme highs" in their life. These moods are called "mania."

There are a few other types of depressive disorders that I will not be addressing here.

Signs and Symptoms of Depression

According to the Anxiety and Depression Association of America, ADAA, and the National Institute for Mental Health (NIMH), there is considerable consensus on the signs and symptoms of depression.

- People experiencing signs of depression for a couple of weeks should seek medical attention. Below are some telling signs and symptoms of depression.

- Persistently sad, anxious, or empty mood.

- Feelings of hopelessness or pessimism.

- Irritability.

- Feeling guilty, meaningless, worthless, or helpless.

- Loss of interest in things previously enjoyed.

- Decreased fatigue or energy.

- Becoming slower in speech or movement.

- Restlessness or trouble sitting still.

- Difficulty in making decisions, concentrating, or remembering easy things.

- Difficult time with sleep, oversleeping, or awakening too early.

- Appetite change or quick weigh change.

- Thoughts of death, suicide, or suicide attempts.

- No clear physical cause for unusual aches, pains, headaches, or digestive problems.

Certainly, not everyone who suffers from the things mentioned is depressed. The severity and frequency of the symptoms are definitely a warning sign.

There are Risk Factors

Depression often occurs during midlife or with older adults. Serious medical conditions can be another critical factor.

Risk factors include:

Some physical illnesses and medications.

A history of family or personal depression.

Trauma, stress, or major changes in a person's life.

Treatment or Therapies

It is important to recognize and understand that there is no "one shoe fits all" when it comes to treatment. At best, it usually requires trial and error to regulate and help those with depression.

Psychotherapies or talk therapy can greatly aid those with depression. There are other types of therapies not listed below, but here are a few of the most common:

There is cognitive-behavioral therapy (CBT).

Interpersonal Therapy (IPT).

Problem-solving Therapy.

Practical Self Treatments

The things that I am going to suggest are not a substitute for going to counseling or going to your physician to seek help. These things are more of something that works along-side your treatment or therapy.

- Determine not to isolate yourself.

- Give yourself time. Moods take time to change.

- Get exercise according to how physically able you are (get your doctor's advice).

- Spend time with people who you love, and you know that they love you.

- Set realistic goals for yourself.

- Learn more about depression.

- Stay encouraged, as this is only a chapter in the book that is your life.

- Postpone major decisions. Decisions such as: moving, marrying, divorcing, having children, or job changes can wait. A person should stop until they are emotionally capable of seeing these things through.

Chapter Eleven

The Ugly Cousin—Suicide

Depression and *suicide* are considered by some, including myself, to be *ugly cousins* that are intricately related to one another. Nevertheless, thankfully, depression does not always lead to suicide. Just as anxiety is a predictor of *depression, depression* itself can predict *suicidal* tendencies.

I shared in the previous chapter how that depression has affected my life. Well, *suicide* has also affected my life and my family. I will give you some personal stories, and then we will discuss what might be going through the suicidal mind. We will also uncover key warning signs, risk factors, and some of the best ways to help someone who may be considering taking their life.

My Family – This Person Lost all Hope

I was getting some clothes out of the dryer in our utility room when my oldest son yelled, "Dad! I just got a phone call from _____ and she said that her mother committed suicide." This person that took their life was very dear to us and was a part of our extended family. The family relationship and the closeness to this tragedy prevent me from revealing more details. To add to the pain, it occurred on my birthday. Thus, my birthday has the potential to be an annual reminder of this heartbreak.

> **THE PAIN OF SOMEONE THAT YOU LOVE, TAKING THEIR LIFE LEAVES AN OPEN EMOTIONAL WOUND.**

It also carves a deep scar on loved ones and friends who suffer from the abrupt loss. There is an indefinite period of time necessary for healing and restoration in the aftermath.

A Pain-Stricken Mother who Lost her Daughter

A few years back, there was a lady who was visiting our church. She had called in advance to make an appointment to speak to me, which demonstrated her eagerness for help. This could either be about a great thing, or something terrible. She shared that the only person that she deeply loved died an unfortunate, untimely death. It was her adult daughter. As we spoke, she revealed that she intended to commit suicide soon. This shook me, but we continued talking for a good while over the phone. Her hope in talking to me was to receive Biblical assurance that if she took her own life, she would not go to hell. I would not grant her wish. Instead, I strongly encouraged her to speak to a doctor and a counselor.

Not long after this conversation, one of our staff members counseled her a couple of times, too. This lady needed professional help that we were unequipped to give her. A lady staff member from our church drove the lady to a professional counseling center. This lady became irate during the counseling session. The counselor called the police for the protection of everyone. Eventually, she was admitted into the psychiatric ward of a general hospital for a couple of days, after which she was released.

Within a few weeks, I received a phone call that this lady had committed suicide. I was extremely saddened to have heard this news despite all our efforts to prevent it. This dear lady had her mind totally set on taking her life, and that is exactly what she did. What could have been done to save her life? I do not know how to answer this question in hindsight; I only wish that we could have done more to help her.

A Struggling Family –
The Wife was Determined to End her Life

A very faithful family in our church was going through some marital issues. There was nothing that could not reasonably be worked out. This couple had been involved for many years together, serving and helping countless people. Gradually, the wife began going through anxiety and depression. She and her husband's relationship began suffering as a result. Eventually, she developed insomnia, so she began taking sleeping pills.

One day, she overdosed on them but was luckily discovered by a loved one in enough time for them to dial 911. The ambulance arrived and carried her to the hospital. The doctors removed the toxic substance from her system. Later that evening, she was dismissed under the supervision of her husband. He took her home. That night, he and the other relative slept lightly. They shared sleeping time between themselves to make sure their loved one was safe and guarded.

In spite of their best attempt to protect her, she managed to sneak past them. The lady went out to their garage, and with the doors tightly shut, she turned on the ignition to their car. She was later found asphyxiated inside due to inhaling too much carbon monoxide. The car was still idling inside the garage filled with exhaust.

A Hurt, Embarrassed and Angry Lady – Determines her Life is Over

This particular day was a disaster for a healthy, promising, young family that was friends of ours. The Saturday began normally for this young mother and wife. The lady's mother came over to the house. There were apparently prior events that led to this grown daughter and her mother into a heated argument. This argument evolved into a physical altercation, and it was rapidly escalating into a nasty situation.

The police were called, and the daughter was taken to jail. While she was in the jail cell, she discovered a way to hang herself. By the time that the jailor found her, she was dead. It appears that hurt, embarrassment, and anger led this sweet person to take her life. She felt that her world had ended and chose death as her escape rather than face it.

What is Going Through a Suicidal Mind?

When I was a boy in depression, I thought about ways that I could die, but I never made any attempts to end my life. In my bouts with depression, I considered suicide as an option at least twice. Nonetheless, I always concluded that suicide would be committing a selfish act by hurting loved ones.

Suicide attempts are almost always rehearsed in a person's mind, usually long before they try to take their life. Tragically, this is especially true for successful suicide attempts as spur-of-the-moment suicide attempts often fail. So, what is going through a persons' mind that is ready to end their life?

- The person feels as though they have completed all their options.

- Their desperation leads them to a dead-end street.

- They have no reason to live - absolutely nothing to live for.

- They want hope, but their fear or their anger closes the door towards better solutions.

- Because Suicide has been a "no-other-best-option" approach, it's their only means with which to stop their emotional pain.

- Sometimes, Suicide is due to substance abuse or chronic pain.

- If it is a psychiatric disorder, the reason might not make reasonable sense.

- Sometimes the person is angry at the world, some other people, and even themselves.

    The attitude can be, "I will show you."

    The attitude can be, "This is what you get for hurting me."

Suicidal Facts

According to the Centers for Disease Control and Prevention (CDC) WISQARS Leading Causes of Death Reports, in 2017:

Suicide was the *tenth* leading cause of death in the United States, claiming the lives of over 47,000 people.

Suicide was the *second* leading cause of death among individuals between the ages of 10 and 34. It is the fourth leading cause of death among individuals between the ages of 35 and 54.

There were more than *twice as many* suicides (47,173) in the United States as there were homicides (19,510).

Psychology Today states that men are at a greater risk than women for suicide. Men's suicidal rate is approximately four times higher.

High-Risk Factors

Who is actually at risk for suicide? Suicide does not discriminate with age, gender, or ethnicity. Remember that it is difficult to predict if or when a person may attempt suicide. So, what are some of the main risk factors of someone ending their life?

Medical illness

Prior suicidal attempts

History of family suicides

Exposure to someone a person loves or admires that committed Suicide

Substance abuse

Depression or some type of mental disorder

Sexual abuse, bullying, physical abuse, or family violence

Being between the ages of 15 – 24 years of age, or over 60 years old

The Centers for Disease Control and Prevention (CDC) states that men are more likely to die by committing suicide than women. Women are more likely to attempt suicide more than men. Men are more likely to use lethal methods of suicide. Women usually attempt suicide by poisoning themselves. There are also demographic factors that I will not address here. You can find this information on the CDC website.

Warning Signs

What should we look out for if someone around us is becoming suicidal?

Mood shifts–

    o Anxiety

    o Extreme anger or irritability

    o Shame

    o Depression

    o Lost care about everything

Talk – The person might discuss, during a serious or sometimes casual conversation, about;

    o Feeling trapped

    o Being a burden to everyone

    o No reason to live

    o Hopelessness

    o Killing themselves

    o Unbearable pain or hurt

Behavior – Changes that are often different due to a painful event, loss, abuse, or bullying.

o Withdrawal or isolation from people or activities they would never want to miss

o Increased usage of drugs or alcohol

o Online research on how to kill oneself

o Sleeping too much or not sleeping enough

o Going to see people they love and basically saying goodbye

o Aggression

o Fatigue

o Giving away precious valuables to people they love

Things We Can Do To Help

If you know of someone who has warning signs or symptoms of suicide, get help immediately. Never tell anyone that you will keep their suicidal thoughts a secret. Many of the social media sites use analytics to identify and report suicidal posts. If you notice anyone posting suicidal messages, call the toll-free National Suicide Prevention Lifeline. Call 1-800-273-TALK (8255) or text the Crisis Text Line (text HOME to 741741) available 24 hours a day, 7 days a week. All calls are confidential to protect the person's anonymity, as well as to make them more comfortable.

The book, *The Worst is Over: What to Say When Every Moment Counts* by Judith Acosta, LCSW, and Judith Simon Prager, PhD., provides basic First Aid Techniques that can be utilized whenever needed. It provides readers with tools beyond just calling for help. You will be equipped to do something on your own, which can be especially useful in the heat of a moment or when key resources are inaccessible. I will share some of these.

Verbal First Aid for Suicide Attempts:

1. Gain rapport with them that is of a special, particular kind. Try to get inside the mind of the person who is close to doing something they cannot come back from - an irreversible act.

2. Detach yourself should you not be able to turn the situation around. This protects and insulates you. As you detach yourself, be loving and kind. Remember that it is not about you. You are not the hero or the zero in the situation at hand.

3. Center yourself as you would in an emergency. Think: Part of me is entering into this person's mind, and part of me is stepping outside my feelings to be useful. Both parts of me pray for guidance and fortune.

Things that I Should not Say:

Never make the mistake of challenging a person who is threatening to commit Suicide.

1. "Go ahead; do it."

2. "Well, it's your choice."

3. "Don't you dare do it."

4. "If you would just read your Bible more."

Any of these statements can seem like a challenge to someone who is on the verge of ending their life. At this point, they are in a delicate state of mind where statements like these might actually encourage them to commit the act. Remember, it is not the size of the problem that the suicidal person is facing. Instead, it is their inability to cope with their life at that moment.

Think of Questions to Keep the Person Talking:

If you can keep them talking for merely one more minute, they may reconsider and step back from their decision.

Be a good listener.

Keep them talking, but do not be irritating.

Avoid saying something true unless it is as simple as, "This is mid-afternoon" or something like that. Saying, "It's a beautiful day," may stir strong emotions in them because they might believe it is an ugly, awful day. Avoid any and all opinions.

Do not force an issue.

The more questions you give answers to, the better you learn how to walk them away from the worst-case consequence.

Apologize if you think it could help.

Sometimes, it will be best to say nothing and just listen.

Be careful not to argue over something.

Here are a few topics suitable to converse with a suicidal individual (Not in any particular order):

"There is always time for suicide," "It's always an option, so you don't have to do it today," "It could be done tomorrow."

"You matter to people." Use anything that you can think of that matters to them. "Who will take care of your dog?" "Who will raise your daughter?"

"What a terrible way to die."

"There is no way back after this."

"What a dismal world this would have been had you never lived." Using a voice of sincerity and strength, communicate to them all the good and positive things that you can think of. Help them understand that these good and positive things would not have happened if they had never been born. Be cautious not to become overenthusiastic, like a cheerleader, because it can seem phony in the heart of someone facing a tragic ending.

"You've made your point, now I understand." This will help them know that you are really, earnestly listening to them. It can be comforting to this person when they know that someone understands them and their plight.

Just do your best, be supportive, and continue in a spirit of prayer. This is the absolute best that you can offer. Forgive yourself if you are unable to rescue someone who chooses death and is unwilling to budge.

Lastly, to reiterate, if you are in the middle of a crisis, call the toll-free National Suicide Prevention Lifeline (NSPL) at 1-800-273-TALK (8255). It is available 24 hours a day, 7 days a week. This service is available to anyone, and all calls are kept strictly confidential.

Chapter Twelve

Survive & Thrive

Part one: Survive – Put the Life Jacket On, Dummy

My Story: Once, I almost drowned in Benbrook Lake

Mark, a friend of mine, hounded me to the point that I finally gave in and went sailing with him. It was my first time to embark on the open seas in a sailboat. I am kidding; it was not the open seas, but a local area lake known as Benbrook Lake.

I did not have any clue whatsoever on what I ought to do, so I trusted Mark to teach me every step of the way. He owned a small sailboat and occasionally took it out for a sail. The boat was the right size for two people, but not one more person than that. Looking back, I think this man understood safe sailing practices marginally.

When we arrived at the lake that day, Mark backed the boat trailer up to the boat ramp. We quickly unloaded the boat, boarded it, and launched out for a leisurely time on the waters. I listened to Mark go on about how this thing called sailing works. For my part, I do not know many of the technical terms for a sailboat. Those who are into this type of sport know all the relevant terminology. You may be that person, and that is great because sailing is an excellent sport. Mark, on the other hand, knew just enough about sailing to make it dangerous for both of us. He used enough sailboat jargon to confuse me thoroughly.

I heard something like this:

Mark: "We want to let the wind drift us to the center of the lake, so I will adjust the sail accordingly. We need the wind to pick up to catch the sail, and it will carry us forward. Once that happens, we will have some fun. So relax and have a nice time. When we get out toward the center of the lake, I will drop anchor, and we can get out of the boat and swim around. Oh yeah, one more thing; if we capsize, do not panic. It is not a big deal. I will need you to swim to one side of the boat, whereas I will swim to the other side. As you grab hold of your side of the boat, pull the boat toward you, and I will push it in your direction from the other side. We will grab the side of the boat and hang on until it turns upright again. Then, we can pull ourselves back into the boat and go for it again. Any questions?"

Me: "Not really... yeah, maybe one question. Don't we need to put on the life-jackets that are lying there on the floor?"

Mark: "No, I never wear those. We will be fine, trust me."

It seemed a bit reckless to me. I was ready for a good time, and I had great respect for bodies of water at the same time. I also knew how to swim fairly well. However, swimming in a large river or lake was quite different than being fifteen or twenty feet away from the ladder on the side of a swimming pool.

I told myself, "Don, stop worrying. This man does this all the time. Be a man, suck it up, and don't be fearful. It's all cool." As I have previously mentioned,

---

I HAVE TO TALK TO MYSELF ABOUT CERTAIN THINGS TO ENCOURAGE MYSELF AND FIND DIRECTION.

Well, we arrived near the center of the lake, dropped anchor, and jumped out of the boat to swim around. We climbed back in and jumped back out. We were laughing and having a fantastic time together. Some time passed, and we climbed back onto the boat. We pulled up the anchor and "set sail" once more. Did you notice how I specifically said, "set sail?"

Mark: "Okay, the wind is moving the water. I think that we can sail now. As I operate the stern, hang on to the hull (which is the side of the boat; see, I do know a couple of sailboat terms) because we will whip back and forth. When you hear the term 'duck,' then duck. Also, don't forget what I told you to do if we capsize. It's not a big deal; I've done it by myself several times. Just hang on to the boat.

Me: "Got it. Let's do this thing!"

Well, I was totally game at this point. The boat had been in the water for some time, and we had also gone swimming. So far, we were having fun.

Off we went on this adrenaline-charged event. I did as I was told. The boat whipped to the left, then quickly to the right, back again to the left, and then right. It was thrilling, but exhausting as well. This went on for a few minutes, and then it happened! In my mind, the unthinkable really happened; we capsized. We flew right into the water headfirst. After I came up to the top, I was only six feet away from the boat.

Mark was yelling, "Grab the boat! Grab the boat!"

Quickly, I swam to the bottom side of the boat, and feverishly struggled to reach the top-side to get a grip. Once I took hold, I clung to the side as Mark worked desperately to untangle the ropes that released the mainsail. I pulled the boat in my direction as he pushed up on the other side. Finally, the boat was restored to its upright position (I am sure there is a correct technical term for that, too).

I was so relieved and drained at the same time. I momentarily removed my hand from the boat. I was treading the water in calm relief when I heard Mark scream: "QUICKLY GRAB THE BOAT! GRAB IT, GRAB THE RUDDER!"

I swam as quickly as I could because the sailboat was speedily drifting away. The rudder was almost in my grasp, or so I thought. I launched myself forward to take hold of the rudder as the boat escaped from my reach. Amazed in disbelief, we were treading water with our mouths dropped wide open. It seemed like the boat was motorized as it was sailing away from us. The ropes never disentangled, and the sails never fell. Thus, the wind caught the sails, causing our ride back to the shore to escape all on its own.

The danger of the moment had not struck yet. I looked over at Mark, who was about six feet from me. He had a look on his face that suggested that "Jaws" was coming after us. Then, he uttered: "Oh no... I'm going to swim away, so we don't drown each other."

As Mark swam away, the terrible position we were in suddenly struck me. In fact, I can almost feel like a panic attack approaching now as I simply relive the occurrence. We were in a desperate situation. I felt a panic attack coming. The water seemed to be crushing my chest, I was taking short breaths, and I was almost unable to breathe.

I quickly spoke aloud, "Don, you can't panic now. This is life or death. You have to pull yourself together. Control your breathing, halt the panic, and get ahold of yourself, man." I kept repeating this to myself, and the thoughts continued for a while.

Mark was about fifty yards away from me as he tried to swim to the shore. I do not know how far from shore that we were. There were no boats in sight, although there was the distant sound of a couple of boats somewhere on the lake.

You may be able to imagine some of the thoughts that were going through my confused, anxious mind.

My first thought was: "This is the way that this happens." All of my life, I've read in the newspaper or heard on the news of people who were healthy, active, good swimmers that unexpectedly drowned for some unknown reason. "Yep, this is the way it happens."

My second thought was: "My wife and my two boys." If I did not make it home, our families and friends would hear of the tragedy. There would be many unanswered questions that would follow soon; the pain and the agony of both of us drowning would be severe for all of them.

My third thought was: "My relationship with God." I knew in my heart that I was a Christian. I had a daily relationship with God, yet it was still scary to think of choking to death alone in the water.

These thoughts, as well as many more, raced through my mind. I could imagine the news, "It is assumed that two men drowned this afternoon in Benbrook Lake. The reasons are unknown. The sailboat that they were in was found upright by someone boating nearby. Their bodies have not yet been found, but area police are searching the lake as I speak." You may not believe that all of this was running through my mind. Yet, there were more thoughts than this tormenting me. One such thought was, "Why didn't you put on the life-jacket?"

I never mentioned what I was wearing. I was wearing a swimming suit, a t-shirt (to avoid sunburn), and a pair of high-top Reeboks (yes, I was stupid). Why did I have on high-top shoes in the boat and in the water? I do crazy things like that. It is a gift.

My shoes felt like heavy, waterlogged sponges. They felt like they weighed 25 pounds each. I knew that I had to remove them, or they would wear me out and weigh me down; I would drown. Unfortunately, the strings were so tight that they were clinging to the shoes, and the shoes themselves were hugging my feet. I kept trying to work them off by rubbing one shoe at a time against my leg.

This did not work, so I tried using my hand to work them off. All of this was to no avail. I took a deep breath and exhaled to calm my nerves. I knew that the only way to remove the high-tops was to take a breath and use both hands to work them off one at a time.

I thought, "Here goes." I took a deep breath and worked off one shoe after an intense struggle. I will never forget the feeling of just dropping the shoe as it fell to the bottom of the lake, thinking, "Don, if you don't make it, that's exactly what is going to happen to you." Letting this one shoe lose encouraged me, and I began working faster and with more determination to remove the other shoe. I dropped it and cringed as it drifted to the bottom. Despite the close call, I felt some success with both shoes off.

I began praying aloud and encouraging myself to keep my focus on surviving. I continued to tread water and pray, then I swam for a short distance. By that time in the late afternoon, the wind had a ripple effect on the water. Small waves suddenly sprung forth, constantly splashing into my mouth and my eyes.

Stuck in the middle of this new chaos, I could still hear Mark yelling in the distance, so I tried the same thing. It seemed like the water was one big acoustic panel that stopped the sound of our voices after about 10 feet. I kept looking toward the closest shoreline where, in the distance, I could make out a few people walking around. They were so far away; they looked like ants crawling on the riverbank. Around thirty minutes had gone by, but it seemed like two hours.

All of a sudden, I was alerted by the sound of a boat somewhere in my vicinity. Looking around, I saw the boat rising over the waterline. Then, I noticed the people on the bank waving their arms around. The boat made its way in that direction, but then I heard the engine die. But after just a few minutes, the boat's engine restarted, and I could see the boat speeding toward the middle of the lake. It appeared they were going in the direction of our sailboat, which I could vaguely see in the distance.

As I kept my eye on the boat, I could see they were nearing Mark's sailboat. Their boat engine's sound slowed down, and when they arrived at the sailboat, they killed the engine completely. It looked like two men, and both were standing up and looking in our boat. Then, I could tell that they began turning in a circle and looking in the water, probably searching for the owners. Both Mark and I were screaming and waving our hands. A moment later, I heard their boat engine start, and they turned around to move in our direction slowly.

The boat slowed down as they approached me, and one man asked:

Man in the boat: "Is that your sailboat?"

Me: "Yes, it is. Can I please get in?"

The man who was controlling the boat seemed somewhat unsure about allowing me to climb onboard. The other guy came over the side of the boat and began assisting me with getting in.

Mark began yelling: "Hurry, I can't take it any longer."

Man, in the boat: "Hold on to the side while we go pick your friend up."

I was hanging on for dear life as they approached Mark. The man who was assisting me went to the other side of the boat. He helped Mark inside, and then he came over and helped me safely onto the boat. It is difficult for me to express how grateful both Mark and I were to these men for saving our lives. They carried us to the sailboat, where it was wobbling back and forth in the water. The guy driving the boat made a smart remark about our life jackets in the boat and us not wearing them. I agreed with him and offered to pay them for their trouble. However, they refused, saying that they did not want any pay.

Mark and I, one at a time, slowly got back into the sailboat and sat down. With both hands, we held on. Both of us were still in shock. Moreover, we were so exhausted that it was almost unbearable to step into the boat. The little sailboat was still wavering on the windswept waves.

We arrived at the boat ramp, loaded the boat, and then headed back home. I do not think we talked to one another as we drove some 40 minutes back to town.

Mark dropped me off at my house and then drove home. As I walked up the sidewalk to my house, my wife opened the door. I have never seen a more beautiful sight. She was standing, holding our three-year-old son. I walked up to them and placed my arms around them. I stood there, crying for a good couple of minutes.

My wife, Kathy, said: "Well, I don't know what happened. I know that something went wrong because you walked up the sidewalk barefooted."

I do rarely go barefooted, even when I am at home. Occasionally, I wear socks around the house, but mostly I wear a pair of socks and shoes. That is who I am. Shoes or no shoes, all of us have to be determined to "survive!" Some events in life will make it almost impossible.

Embrace the Key Survival Elements for your Life

1. Learn to speak to yourself when a panic attack arrives.

2. Walk through the attack.

3. STAY IN THE MOMENT!

4. Continue to encourage yourself.

5. Fight through the attack.

6. Do not fight against the attack, but fight through the attack. SURVIVE!

7. Don't wear high-top shoes in the river and don't be dumb; wear a lifejacket!

Part Two – Have a Plan and Work your Plan

My Story: Doing the Right Thing, Moving On to a New Plan for my Life

I'm not the brightest light bulb in the box; I assume that you have already identified that characteristic.

I have made so many mistakes and bad decisions in my life, and yes, it does hurt.

You have read many of my personal stories about my anxiety disorder, panic attacks, and depression:

Now, digest this:

I have not given up, and I continue with a vision for life. I have a plan to "survive and thrive."

Near the conclusion of the 25 years of being the pastor of a life-giving church, I had endured depression. The depression occurred at several intervals.

The last episode of depression existed for around four years. During the last year in my position as pastor, I had become emotionally numb. I had lost the emotions of joy and fun and had developed an inability to shed tears. This was not me, and I decided that I could not live in that condition any longer. I felt as though I was dishonest. I was not living properly in this frame of mind, as I served the church that I had loved and ministered, for a quarter of a century. Something had to be done, but this was a huge life-changing decision to make. This decision would affect my family, as well as several thousand people.

My psychiatrist carefully supervised the Zoloft medication that he had prescribed me. Before I decided to resign from my position, I desired to work my way off of the medication. Understand that I am not recommending anyone reading this to stop taking medication. At the end of the day, that is medication your doctor has prescribed for you, and they are qualified physicians.

This was something that I knew in the depths of my heart that I should do; it is not my recommendation for you or anyone else for that matter. Under the supervision of my doctor, I gradually worked my way off of Zoloft. I have nothing against Zoloft. In fact, for a while, I needed to take it.

It took me over one month to become free from medication. This was the most difficult decision that I have ever had to make. I had to resign as lead-pastor, even though this was a position I held for over 25 years. The decision was made after I processed it past my family, as well as the leadership of the church. I followed this with an official resignation to the congregation in November 2006.

What would I do now? In an earlier chapter, I explained some things that I did. That, however, does not explain how I arrived at where I am currently in life. I had been praying, "God, what is it that you want me to do. Please show me your plan."

I wholeheartedly believe that God has a unique plan for every person's life. It does not matter how brief one's life may be or how long a person lives. If you and I are breathing air, then there is a plan for us. We are not here to waste space.

At this point, I want to explain something crucial to you. For around nine months, I had been seeking and praying about the type of ministry I could lead. I came up with a list of five things and listed them in the order of my desires from first to last. Here was my list:

1. Get a secular job, go to a church, and serve in some capacity on Sunday.

2. Serve as a staff pastor in some church bi-vocationally. That means having a secular job, as well as a church pastor's job on a part-time basis.

3. Be a foreign missionary. My wife and I even applied and interviewed with a major denomination to serve as foreign missionaries. We decided to withdraw our application before going before the national mission board, due to a variety of complicated reasons.

4. I considered becoming the lead pastor of a church somewhere. That church would have to be the perfect fit to not be crossed off of my list.

5. Be a part of planting a new church somewhere. I would not be the lead pastor, though.

Here is what took place:

I was working at the construction company that I had mentioned in an earlier chapter. I happened to have two friends from different venture points in my life. The two men did not know one another, but both had contacted me with a keen interest in planting a new church in the metroplex area. I decided to introduce these men to one another. I hoped that perhaps they could work together to achieve their dreams of founding a new church. I wanted them to stop constantly pestering me about starting a church.

So I came up with a plan and invited these two men with their wives to have dinner with my wife and me. One of my friends requested to bring along another friend of his, too. So his friend and his wife joined the six of us for dinner one evening. After dinner that night, one of my friends invited all of us over to their house. We agreed to go, and all eight of us visited them for a couple of hours.

I did not talk much that night because I wanted them to talk and share their thoughts and dreams of starting a new church. I was ready to leave for a good while, so finally, I motioned for my wife to start getting ready to head home. Before I made my move, the gentleman, who was the new acquaintance, asked if he could say something to me. I will call him George. Despite how late it was, I agreed to listen:

George: "Don, you don't know me, and you may get uncomfortable after hearing me say some things that are on my mind. You can get up and leave if you wish, or you may want to punch me right in the face."

He proceeded to explain how he felt compelled to disclose to me how the entire evening that night was not about any of them. The night together was exclusively for me. He shared some things about me that were true. Basically, he explained where he thought that I was in my life. He continued to speak about what it would take to move me into the place that I was looking for. This was really crazy, as this gentleman shared his discernment about my life. I think he talked for about 30 minutes. It soon became apparent that he had been observing me all evening.

When he was finished talking, I promptly thanked him, as well as the others. Afterward, my wife and I promptly left their house and got into our car. We sat in the car for a few moments, and my wife remarked, *"Well, it sounded like that man had your number tonight."* I did not like what she had to say, nor what the man had to say. My wife and I quickly commenced our short 30-minute drive home and remained quite most of the way. I was upset and did not want to talk, something which she had intuitively sensed.

To shorten the story, the man was right. I accepted that there was something that I was supposed to do. Surprisingly, "that thing" so happened to be number five on the list of things that I would be willing to do. It was not number one, two, three, or four. Number five was God's plan for Kathy and me. Planting a new church and becoming its lead-pastor, was a stretch of the last thing that I wanted to do. It was quite crazy in hindsight. Thinking back to that night almost twelve years ago makes me appreciate how momentous it was. I felt God giving me the message, "Go to Crowley, Texas, and share your story." That is what we did, and we are still doing that to this day.

I will not go into detail about planting a new church. A small group of individuals gradually gathered around me. We developed a church "startup team." This team consisted of around fifty people to set up, take down, teach, lead worship, and love people. A plan was developed to begin the church with two pre-services and then launch in the third month. On our first pre-service, over 180 people showed up. That was a fantastic beginning, but it was also the lowest attended service that the church has ever had.

We began in a public school in Crowley, Texas, where the church met weekly for over three years. After that, we moved to a shopping center and remodeled it to fit the church's needs. We are currently in the same location. Our church is The Fountains Fellowship Church, Crowley, Texas, and we also have a second church campus in Fort Worth, Texas. Both churches provide a complimentary café, nursery – fifth-grade children's classes, a worship team, and live preaching.

On Wednesday nights, we minister to scores of teenagers with games, food, small groups, and a worship service. God has given us a group of sacrificing, amazing people who get the job done. On both of our campuses, we attempt to reach out to the community to extend love, life, and hope to the hopeless. We have seen hundreds of lives change for the better, and we continue to "share our story."

A Plan to Survive and Thrive

Have you ever asked someone, "Hey, how are you doing?" and this person replies, "I am alright under the circumstances." Once, I heard someone answer in response to that response, "Well, what are you doing under the circumstances. Get out from underneath those things." I have learned that we must have a determined mindset, no matter what, even with an anxiety order.

I am going to list some things that will enable most people to "survive and thrive." Take these or encourage someone with anxieties to move forward in life. Stop making excuses, and you can progress into a better place in life. A new place of fulfillment and of your calling, whatever you sense that to be.

- Cope, do not mope. I have mentioned this before, and it is important to be heading toward the good things in your life.

- Remember that you will "feel the way that you think." Be careful what you are feeling; change your feelings. Remember to control your mind, and do not allow it to control you.

- Keep in mind that "sadness is not depression." Each of us will have our sad times or sad days. Get positive and work these ideas into your life.

STAY IN THE MOMENT. Do not think about the last time the panic attack came. Keep your focus on NOW.

- *Stay away from addictions.* Any of us can become addicted to almost anything. Addictions range from alcohol, pharmaceuticals, sex, TV, Movies, the internet, games, tobacco, marijuana, pain killers, cocaine, heroin, gambling, shopping, or food. Are you ready for me to stop? The bottom line is, avoid all addictions.

- *Visualize success.* Discipline yourself to see that you will have the opportunities to succeed to be the best that you can be.

You and I have this one life to live. Let the past be the past. Begin doing the things you have always wanted to today, no matter how small, to begin shaping positive results. The things that will bring you physical and emotional health and well-being are always worth the time, resources, and investment.

It is only natural to go after what you want in life. Do not club yourself into any of this. Dream, and then learn all that you can about what you want to do and what you want to be. Take baby steps to avoid overwhelming yourself. Learn to respect yourself. If you do not respect yourself, you cannot expect others to respect you, either. Endorse yourself!

IT IS ALL ABOUT HABIT MANAGEMENT.

This has enabled me to reach many extraordinary goals in life, and if I can do it, you can do it as well. Find someone that you love and respect, and ask them to keep you accountable. You can do this, and you will find out that it will be worth your efforts. You will begin feeling good about yourself. I believe in you. God believes in you. I know that you care about yourself, too, or you would not have read this book to this point. Allow me to add one more thought: If this book has been a blessing to you – pass it on, share it with someone. You can make a big difference in a person's life. **Have a Blessed Life - Survive and Thrive!**

Bibliography

Chapter 1

Davis, Kim. "Anxiety: What An Individual May Be Experiencing or Feeling." *Indiana Resource Center for Autism*, IU Bloomington, Retrieved 9 June, 2019. http://iidc.indiana.edu.

"Mindfulness." *Google Dictionary*, Retrieved 23 July, 2019.

Wehrenberg, Margaret. *The 10 Best-Ever Anxiety Management Techniques*: New York, London, W.W. Norton Publishers, second edition, 2018.

Sifferlin, Alexandria. "How You Deal With Your Emotion Can Influence Your Anxiety." *Healthland Times*, Retrieved 10, June, 2019.

Ross, Franzi, "Stress vs. Anxiety – Knowing The Difference Is Critical to Your Health." *Anxiety News*, Retrieved 8 June, 2019.

"What are the Five Major Types of Anxiety Disorders?" *HHS.gov Answers*. U.S. Department of Health and Human Services, Retrieved 28 May, 2019.

Chapter 2

Burns, David. *Feeling Good: The New Mood Therapy*. New York: Harper Collins Publishers, 1980.

"History." *LDA Learning Disabilities Association of America,* Retrieved 8 July, 2019. http://www.idaamerica.org/about-us/history/

Morin, Amanda. *A Timeline of Learning and Attention Issues,* Understood.org USA LLC, 2014.

Chapter 3

"AADA Anxiety and Depression Association of America." *Depression,* Retrieved 18 June 2019.

"AADA Anxiety and Depression Association of America." *Facts,* Retrieved 18, June 2019.

"AADA Anxiety and Depression Association of America." *Highlights: Workplace Stress and Anxiety Disorders Survey,* Retrieved 30 May, 2019.

Mc Donach, Barry. *DARE.* San Bernardino: BMD Publishing LTD, 2015.

Smith, Kathleen. "Work Anxiety: 10 Tips To Manage Anxiety At Work," *Psycom.net,* Retrieved 30 May, 2019.

Chapter 4

"AADA Anxiety and Depression Association of America." *Depression,* Retrieved 19 June, 2019.

Concic, Arlin. "How Generalized Anxiety Disorder Can Affect Your Relationships." *Verwellmind.com,* Retrieved 7 May, 2019.

Erhart, Laura. "Me, My, Anxiety and My Marriage." *The Chill Times*, Retrieved 3 June, 2019.

Greco, Carla. "Anxiety, Depression and Your Marriage." *Hitchmag.com*, Retrieved 3 June, 2019.

Partridge, Dale. "How Anxiety Almost Destroyed My Marriage." *The Daily Positive.com*, Retrieved 3 June, 2019.

Tango, Your. "How I Stay Happily Married to a Man With Anxiety." *Huffpost.com*, News Media Website, 29 June, 2016, Retrieved 3 June, 2019.

Chapter 5

Burns, David. *"Feeling Good: The New Mood Therapy."* New York: Collins Harper Publishers, 1980.

Boyes, Alice. *"The Anxiety Toolkit."* New York: The Penguin Group (USA) LLC. 2015.

Chapter 6

Burns, David. *"Feeling Good: The New Mood Therapy."* New York: Collins Harper Publishers, 1980.

Mc Donach, Barry. *DARE.* San Bernardino: BMD Publishing LTD, 2015.

"Only thing we have to fear is fear itself." *FDR's First Inaugural Address.* History Matters. Gmu.edu., Retrieved 29 May, 2019.

Ross, Franzi, "Stress vs. Anxiety-Knowing The Difference is Critical to Your Health." *Anxiety News*. Retrieved 8 June, 2019.

Chapter 7

Boyes, Alice. *"The Anxiety Toolkit."* New York: The Penguin Group (USA) LLC. 2015.

Handel, Steven. "How To Build Thick Skin And Stop Being So Sensitive." *The Emotion Machine*, 27 February, 2014, Retrieved 6 June, 2019.

Leaver, Kate. "The Rise of Workplace Anxiety (And How to Cope)." *Glamourmagazine.co.uk*. Retrieved 22 June, 2019.

Mc Donach, Barry. *DARE*. San Bernardino: BMD Publishing LTD, 2015.

Wehrenberg, Margaret. *The 10 Best-Ever Anxiety Management Techniques*: New York, London, W.W. Norton Publishers, second edition, 2018.

Chapter 8

Andriana. "Bitterness, Anxiety and Three Other Things To Get Rid of Today." *aloveworthylivingfor.com*, Retrieved 20 June, 2019.

Burns, David. *"Feeling Good: The New Mood Therapy."* New York: Collins Harper Publishers, 1980.

Diamond, Stephen and Messina, James. "Don't Let Your Anger 'Mature' into Bitterness." *Anger Maturing into Bitterness*, 14, January 2015, Retrieved 10 June, 2019.

Maridable, Peter. "The Surprising Emotion Behind Anxiety." *Psychologytoday.com*, 25 July, 2016, Retrieved 25 July, 2019.

Resentment. http://www.vocabulary.com/dictionary/bitter, Retrieved 17 June, 2019.

Stosny, Steven. "Anger-How we Transfer Feeling of Guilt, Hurt and Fear." *Psychologytoday.com*, 14 June, 2014, Retrieved 10 June, 2019.

Warren, Rick. "Rick Warren: People are Irritable Because They are Hurt." *CP Church and Ministries*, Retrieved 6 July, 2019.

Wolfe, David. "Bitter People Have These 5 Habits." *Avoid Them.* David Wolfe.com, Retrieved 19 June, 2019.

Chapter 9

The Bible, *The New International Version*. Nashville, Broadman and Holman Publishers. 1996.

Dymski, Rachael. "What my Anxiety Taught Me About God." *Revelantmagazine.com*, Retrieved 12 June, 2019.

Graber, Don. "Anxiety Disorders -Frequently Asked Questions." *Focusonthefamily.com*, Retrieved 12, June, 2019.

Padilla, Joe. "What the Bible Says About Depression and Anxiety." *Mentalhealthgracealliance.org*, Retrieved 12 June, 2019.

Zigler, Zig. *See You At The Top*. Gretna: Magna Publishing Co Ltd; first edition. 2005.

Chapter 10

AADA "Anxiety and Depression Association of America." *Signs and Symptoms*, Retrieved 30 May, 2019.

AADA "Anxiety and Depression Association of America." *Risk Factors, Treatments and Therapies*, Retrieved 30 May, 2019.

Burns, David. *"Feeling Good: The New Mood Therapy."* New York: Collins Harper Publishers, 1980.

Depression. "Signs and Symptoms." *National Institute of Mental Health*, Nimh.nih.gov, Retrieved 12 June, 2019.

Depression "322 Million People." *Ourworld Data*, AADA.org, Retrieved 12 June, 2019.

Mc Allister, Dawson. "Understanding Depression." *The Hopeline.com*, Retrieved 24 May, 2019.

Chapter 11

Acosta, Judith and Prager, Judith. *The Worst is Over*. San Diego: Jodere Group, 2002.

Burns, David. *"Feeling Good: The New Mood Therapy."* New York: Collins Harper Publishers, 1980.

"Centers for Disease Control." *Violence Prevention.* www.cdc.go/violenceprevention/suicide/index/html.

Leading Causes of Death, Centers for Disease Control and Prevention, *WISQARS*, Retrieved 17 June, 2019.

National Suicide Prevention Lifeline. *Suicide Prevention*, Preventionlifeline.org, Retrieved 22 June, 2019.

Markaway, Barbara. "20 Expert Tactics for Dealing with Difficult People." *Psychologytoday.com*, 3 May, 2015, Retrieved 10 June, 2019.

What is Suicide" *National Institute of Mental Health*, Retrieved 12 June, 2019.

Who Is At Risk For Suicide: *National Institute of Mental Health*, 12 June, 2019.

Suicide. "The Facts on Suicide." *Psychologytoday.com*, Retrieved 12 June, 2019.

Chapter 12

Burns, David. *"Feeling Good: The New Mood Therapy."* New York: Collins Harper Publishers, 1980.

Wehrenberg, Margaret. *The 10 Best-Ever Anxiety Management Techniques*: New York, London, W.W. Norton Publishers, second edition, 2018.